Death Grip on the Pommel:
A Warrior's Journey to Grace

Also by
John Myerson and Judith Robbins

Voices From the Other Side of the Couch
A Warrior's View of Shamanic Healing

Also co-authored by
John Myerson
with
Jay Thomas

Riding the Spirit Wind
Stories of Shamanic Healing

©Copyright 2011 John G. Myerson and Judith Robbins
All rights reserved. No part of this book may be used or reproduced in any form or by any means, electronic or mechanical, including photocopying and recording, or by any information storage and retrieval system, without the permission in writing from the publisher.

For inquiries:
LifeArts Press
WayoftheRedDragon.com.
Printed in the United States of America
Cover art ©Copyright 2011 Millyard Design. All rights reserved.
For more info go to www.millyarddesign.com

First Edition 2011
Paperback ISBN: 978-0-9816420-8-6
eBook ISBN: 978-0-9816420-5-5
Death Grip on the Pommel: A Warrior's Journey to Grace
John G. Myerson and Judith Robbins

PLEASE NOTE
The cases described in this book are composites. They have been deliberately combined and altered in order to protect John Myerson's patients' rights of confidentiality and privacy.

No one found in this book corresponds to any actual person, living or dead.

DEDICATED TO

*The Healing Circle,
Our first Way of Power Group,
For all the love, support and
healing along the Way.*

Acknowledgments

Life is supported and nurtured by the community that surrounds us. We have been particularly fortunate in that regard. Humbly and profoundly, we would like to thank all those who have given to us for this project. Without you, none of this would be possible.

Thanks to all of John's patients who have shared their souls with him. He is very honored to be able to be present for this.

Thanks to all of the members of the LifeArts Way of Power groups. These training groups are the building blocks of our community. We are honored to be able to be a part of this extraordinary group of people on the Way.

Special thanks to the members of the LifeArts Nei Gung group: John Demarco, Michael Short, Lee Taylor, and Jon Woodward. It takes a unique person to connect with John in this arena. Your work has contributed to this book in so many ways that they are impossible to enumerate.

We would like to express our thanks to Harry and Marjorie Millyard of Millyard Design for their kindness in cover design/illustration and typesetting of this book.

Thanks to all our readers: Deb Adcock, Elizabeth Frankl, Patty Gibbons, and Anne Keaney. Your input was greatly appreciated.

Special thanks to David Myerson for his input from his "unique perspective."

Extra special thanks go to Judy Seidl. Her love was essential to the making of this book.

From John: thanks to the men—Bruce Berlent, Andy Osborne, Peter Ostrow, Mark Halperin, and Paul Weisman. For nineteen years and counting, you have been there for me, week after week. I appreciate your love and support more than you can imagine. To Christine Lee for her love, compassion, and healing. To my dear friend John Shelton for his love, support, and positive energy. To Jan Hastings, for being you. To Patty Gibbons for your beautiful energy and connection.

As always to my wife, Laura. You who keep me grounded in the world. All my love.

From Judy: love and gratitude to Stanton, Denise, Ben, and Rachel, who bring light and love. To Anne for friendship, laughter, and kindness. To the reading group for stimulating the mind and offering understanding and support over the years. To the Myerson/Talmud Clan for their friendship, perception, warmth, and wisdom. To Martin, who taught me about the creative life, among other things.

Contents

Acknowledgments	vii

Introduction	1
Doing and Being	5
The Balance of Doing and Being	15
Ho'o Pono Pono	23
Ariel	33
Vesta	47
Discipline	57
Resistance I	69
Resistance II	81
Aphrodites	85

Resistance III	93
Brother Hawk	99
The Gift	107
Rhiannon	113
Death Grip on the Pommel	117
Works Cited	119
Suggested Readings	121
About the Authors	129

Introduction

When people first come to my office, their impression is of a quiet, comfortable space. There are colorful Southwestern rugs on the floor, Navajo and Japanese calligraphy wall hangings, a dimly illuminated pink quartz stone, and pictures of my family. I sit across from them in my big, embracing black chair. I'm built big and powerful, but the impression, I'm told, is of a calm, kind, receptive man who laughs a lot. There's truth to that, but what most people don't know is the long struggle I've had with a powerful, instinctive impulse toward violence.

I've had to face this impulse in my work as a healer. Obviously, violence and healing don't go together easily. Yes, sometimes I can use my warrior nature shamanically to protect a patient, but I've had to learn balance and make peace with this violent ability to support and help others. When I sit down with someone, I draw on my training in Oriental medicine, psychology, Buddhism, Taoism, and shamanism, whatever seems most useful. My goal is to help people develop their unique gifts and abilities to heal. To do so, I've had to learn to use love. Hard as it has been to change, I learn from the history of others who have evolved from violence to healing—not an easy path but one I have undertaken.

As an example of the quick flaring of violence that I've worked hard to get free of, let me tell you of an incident that took place thirty years ago. I was visiting my friend Sam when another friend, Raul, suggested that he and I do some pushing hands. This can be a rather harmonious exercise, just shifting weight back and forth, keeping contact with forearms and hands, sensing and testing each other's balance.

"Sure, whatever," I said, not knowing that they had a plan to goad me into action.

Raul and I did a little bit, then more. Suddenly he tried to get through my guard. He stepped in and struck right at me with his fist. Instantly my yang energy came up, and I wanted to kill him—not just emotionally, I really wanted to kill him. My reaction was split-second and instinctive. I sank to get him leaning into me, and when I had his energy, I used it against him in a move called "receiving energy." Instantly he was in the air and ten feet across the room, splatted against the wall, the way you see in cartoons. I moved toward him, wanting to put him through another wall, a look in my eye like a hawk diving toward prey. Fortunately, I stopped so as not to hurt him. Later, however, I got sick because I'd had all that energy roused up and held it back, didn't discharge it.

I thought, "There has to be a better way."

This book is about my finding that better way. I'm still a warrior, and I still use dark energy to help and protect when it's called for, but there's no longer that ferocity, that violence. How did I do this? It's been a long road.

I've learned that balancing one's energy is the way to go, and for me using discipline was the way to achieve a kind of balance. This balance took different forms as I explored. The first chapter, for example, describes how I, someone who's instinctually geared toward action, toward what I call Doing, learned also to cultivate an opposite state, which I call Being. You may think about which way you lean and consider trying to find your own balance between the two.

In other chapters, I try to show the way I learned to use loving energy, the different ways I saw what balance meant, the reason discipline is so crucial, and finally the deepest insight and experiences, which have changed the way I am and the way I am with others.

The organization is roughly sequential, indicating the progression I went through because it's my story, but each section may be of use in itself. I hope you will find something helpful to you in your own quest for whatever balance you need.

Doing and Being

As I thought about what was going on to create such violence in me, one of my first insights was to distinguish between Doing and Being. At this stage, I then thought about ways to balance these two modes.

Doing and Being are opposite expressions of energy, like yin/yang, light/dark, male/female. The energy of the Universe is one. In other words, it is just energy. We rarely experience the pure single energy of the Universe though we read or hear accounts of ecstatic experiences of unity, maybe even are gifted with such a singular experience ourselves. In the realm of conscious reality—our ordinary reality—this energy of the Universe is expressed and perceived as two or a duality. We do tend to think in terms of categories. When a baby is born, one of the first questions is, "Is it a boy or a girl?" We think of actions as good or evil, and so on.

For our purposes in this discussion of balance, I will use the contrasting modes of Doing and Being as another way the energy of the Universe is expressed as two different realities in our ordinary lives.

To begin, let me explain Doing by describing my work as a warrior healer. When someone comes into my office, I can see when he is possessed by a spirit, or I can see a darkness around him, or I can see a seductive woman draining him. In such cases, I can protect someone by defeating and clearing darkness, or by separating souls. Here I use a direct energy to act as the kind of warrior who attacks whatever is causing harm.

My focus is external, and the action is linear. I focus, I see, and I attack. Here I am Doing.

Another way to explain what I mean by Doing is to describe one way I do martial arts. I've developed my own form of internal martial arts that I call LifeArts Nei Gung. It focuses on learning how to move with the energy of the Universe through sparring. When I practice this with my co-learners, they're accustomed to my coming at them with the old kind of warrior approach. In this mode, I focus my concentration on my opponent very intently. I look at him very carefully, using the third eye, hyperfocusing. It becomes a multi-sensory experience—feeling, seeing, hearing energy patterns, sensing what he is going to do.

I'm like the two swordsmen in an old Japanese story. These two masters met to fight a serious match. They stood and stared at each other for an hour. Then one just bowed, and they went home. By reading each other's energy in this intense way, they knew all they needed to know to realize who would win the match.

When I'm sparring as this kind of warrior, I generate energy and send it out at my opponent. This kind of energy is clear, cold, non-emotional, and hard energy. It cuts and has a sharp edge. The guys in my class tell me that when I focus at them this way, I look like pictures of the Boddhidharma, fierce, ferociously concentrated.

When an opponent has some tightness in his knee, hip, or mind, I sense it and my energy directs right to it, the energy around me will focus on that tightness, and he'll get off balance.

My sparring technique has been to get my partner to resist; then he's on the defensive, and I can get him.

One great example of this kind of warrior is Morihei Ueshiba, a Japanese master who lived in the late nineteenth and early twentieth centuries. He fascinates me because in his early period he was a crazy warrior; he would train all day, practice a sword strike thousands of times until he mastered it. He would challenge anyone, kill people, and throw them around the room if they just looked at him the wrong way.

In my earlier days, I identified with Ueshiba, loved to throw people around, and was fierce with the sword though I never hurt anyone with more than bruises. What happens is that a vibration builds and builds in me, and then it needs to be released—and it comes out hard and fast. I go forward, forward, come at an opponent. My opponents feel scared because they feel a wall of energy coming at them and know I'm going to hit.

When I was younger, the energy would build up to a point where I couldn't control it, and it would come out violently. Now I have better control, and I can just stand there and exude that Doing energy. When I am in this space, an opponent can't do anything to me.

Maintaining this warrior energy is, however, very tiring. When I used it exclusively, all my energy was going out. I saw that Doing leaves a trace, like fine ash. It is like dust on a mirror. The more I would do, the more the ash would build up on the mirror. When I used my energy to attack, even if I was doing so to help and protect, it took from me. Sometimes I would get sick after using this Doing energy intensely.

So, I started to wonder whether there wasn't a way to achieve some balance, a way to be powerful without focusing only on winning, beating, and destroying. If there was this yang aggressive way, there had to be a yin way. There had to be a way to clean the mirror.

This search for balance led me to explore what I call Being, a mode explored in internal martial arts, in Buddhism and Taoism.

When I'm in Being mode, instead of focusing out intensely, I let my breath relax. I let go of focus and feel as if energy is coming into me, as if it just flows into me. There are waves of energy that I call on to direct me. I'm not directing it. Doing takes a lot of one's own energy to hyperfocus and maintain the hyperfocus. Being is a letting go of one's own energy. The energy is supplied and rushes in. Doing is about protection, the outer. Being is about love, the inner healing.

Here's how Being feels: I feel my body vibrating, so fine and fast that others can't see it. Then that vibration takes over my body. Think of a tuning fork resonating to the vibrations of another tuning fork; it feels as if the vibration and I are moving together, but I don't think about it; it just happens. I'm just moving with it. Even while I'm just talking about this, my hands start to move in waves and my body starts to sway.

When this happens, I feel as if I am a tuning fork, but not just for one note. It's a series of patterns of notes. The vibrations change depending on what's around me, what the patient needs, and what the opponent does.

Sparring from Being is different from sparring from Doing. I was first introduced to internal Chinese martial arts in 1970 and was immediately attracted to them. Although I had studied and would continue to study external styles for years to come, the idea of being with the flow of the Universe led me to fall in love with these internal systems, a love affair that continues to this day.

My sparring partners say that when I'm in Being mode, instead of scowling fiercely with concentration, I have a big grin on my face. Paradoxically, they also say that when I'm in this mode, I'm even scarier than when in Doing mode. Why? Because with Doing they can see and feel what's coming at them. Here, with Being, the energy is warm and welcoming. I'm not projecting out at them; I'm just being with the warm flow.

I'm making myself vulnerable and welcoming them in. They feel as if they're being sucked into a spider web or the vacuum of a black hole, and they don't know what's going on.

A great practitioner of this method was T. T. Liang, a twentieth-century Tai Ch'i master. Unlike the ferocious young Ueshiba, T. T. would greet you with a friendly "nice to see you." I never saw him hurt anyone, and he'd kid back and forth, laugh at you and always say nice things (because, he said, "they can't come back at you"). This manner belied his ability, though.

Once, I went to visit him with my teacher at the time, Leung Kay-Chi, son-in-law of a Shaolin master, with whom I'd work out using a huge iron spear. Leung was deferential to T.T. because the Tai Chi master was so much older. After we'd had tea and talked for a bit, Leung decided to push hands with T. T., who shuffled like an old man, which he was. Leung took a fierce low bow stance and got centered and balanced. T. T. made a small movement and sent the younger man flying.

Interestingly, the fierce Ueshiba came to Being mode also. He had enlightenment experiences which convinced him that "the essence of Aikido is to put oneself in tune with the functioning of the Universe. Those who have grasped the inner meaning of Aikido possess the Universe within themselves" (Stevens, *Abundant Peace*, 112). Toward the end of his long life, he said, "martial artists who are not in harmony with the Universe are merely executing combat techniques" (Stevens, *Abundant Peace*, 112). At this point, he was able to subdue an opponent with one finger.

To illustrate by way of contrast, another great warrior and martial arts master, Yamaoka Tesshu, was not able to calm his energy completely. Like Ueshiba, he was highly disciplined—in his warrior practice (swordsmanship every day from six in the morning until nine), in his calligraphy (from ten until four or five), and in his practice of Zen meditation (often past midnight) (Stevens, *Sword of No Sword*, 76). In fact, he achieved enlightenment. But he said that until he was forty-nine, he was not able to "transcend sexual passion," and before that had sex with thousands of women ("hoping to bridge the gap between man and woman, self and other") (Stevens, *Sword of No Sword*, 66). He was also a prodigious and joyous drinker until the end of his life.

My interpretation is that he needed the sex and the drinking to cool, to dissipate, the intense yang energy he created. He died at fifty-three. Ueshiba died at eighty-six. John Stevens, learned biographer of both men, concluded, "In my view it is Tesshu who teaches the budoka how to 'live completely' and Morehei [Ueshiba] who shows us the actual methods of embracing opposition with love" (Stevens, *Abundant Peace*, 122).

The idea of embracing opposition with love shows in two ways in my Nei Gung group. First, here's how it manifests in the actual sparring. When we use the Being mode, a person will put his hand on his partner's chest and slowly push it. When my partner pushes me, I don't actually move. The process is internal. I open my heart, so there's no fear; I'm inviting him in, not resisting him.

The energy goes down my back leg into my heel. The energy feels as if it's being packed, rather like pushing down on a spring. My partner feels as if he's being sucked in, or as if he's falling off a cliff. Then he's overextended, falling. When the spring can't pack any more, I release it and he goes poof. Again, this is an internal movement of energy, not an external movement.

One week, my partner and I were trying to relax any resistance we could feel on any level, physical, emotional, mental, or spiritual. The energy rushed in and directed us, we didn't direct it. There was beautiful energy between us. From the outside, we looked like two old men moving slowly doing some kind of weird dance. Inside, it felt as if we were both connected to an energy wave and being moved by it.

The second manifestation of Being in the Nei Gung group comes in the way I see teaching and learning. The goal is to have each person achieve the highest level he can. It's not for me as a teacher to show how good I am or to be better than everyone else. In fact, if I help others with this communal intent, I get better myself. As any teacher knows, students challenge you to grow and learn. So often in martial arts, and elsewhere, for that matter, things are hierarchical. The teacher has his or her best disciples; then the disciples have their students and so on down the line until doctrines get interpreted, distorted, or fossilized. I want none of that. When students ask me about earning different belts, I laugh and say, "Sure, just go to the store and buy whatever you want."

I just want all to be able to connect to the power of the Universe for themselves. One of my favorite sayings is, "If a student has not equaled or surpassed the teacher, both have failed." So, I don't want to Do, act aggressively to make myself superior. I want to Be, so as to encourage all to find their connections to each other and to the Universe.

I'm also using the Being mode in my work as a healer. Instead of what one seer called my old tendency to just act fast, now I try to pause, stop, and let myself be in a Being place first. I don't do anything, I just watch. If I feel as if I'm called to do something, then it's God or the Spirit or the Universe [whatever you call it doesn't matter] that comes through me and does the healing. I'm like a conduit and don't deplete my own energy.

I've learned to resist the temptation to jump in quickly when a patient wants me to heal her. Even if I wanted to take over and cure a patient, though I might help her, I can't make the change she needs for her. Think of an analogy to working with an alcoholic. You can't make her stop. If you jump in and rescue her when she doesn't want to change, you're enabling her. In addition, if I do try to take over and do the work for the patient, my energy is going out. Before I understood this, my energy would be depleted, and I'd get sick all the time. I remember one six-month period when I got pneumonia three times.

I have a patient who's not doing well physically or emotionally. She won't see a doctor and claims I'm the only one who can heal her. She thinks that everything is a battle, that the forces of evil are invading, so she wants me to come in with my sword. It used to be that I'd think, yes, I need to step in and help, to save her. Now warning bells go off.

She is a dark Aphrodite [more about Aphrodites later], one who will feed off the energy of others until they are sick and burned out; then she will go on to someone else. If she can't find others, she will get sick. Because I looked and waited, I saw this pattern. First, I saw that there wasn't anything evil around her, so this was all in her head, not that she didn't really believe it. If there had been a need for me to come in and ward off a real danger, I'd have seen that and then moved to Doing mode.

What did I do? I gave her a book on Ho'o Pono Pono [a practice which proposes a Being and loving approach; more about that later too] and I disappeared psychically so that she couldn't find me.

I've described Doing and Being as distinct, in an effort to make them clear. In practice, they may get combined. One isn't either a Do-er or a Be-er. There's a flow of yin and yang, back and forth. Think of how you can move your hands in a circular way to make an energy ball, constantly shifting, trying to find the balance, knowing when to use one motion or the other.

In a given situation, I may use either or both. There aren't clear-cut steps of when to use Being and when to use Doing. You just go with what you perceive. That's your starting point, and you have to maneuver from there. You have to sense what is needed and keep your balance as you flow between Being and Doing.

This understanding was the first major step in my learning about balance as a way to ease my tendency to jump to a Doing and often violent response.

The Balance of Doing and Being

In the last chapter, I tried to explain two ways of using energy—Doing and Being. By thinking about and using this duality, I've been able to balance the two as needed in various situations. Most important, balancing them has helped me overcome my tendency to tip too far into Doing and violence.

I hope that what I've learned can be useful to others also, so here I'd like to pause and consider how you might try to balance Being and Doing in ways that work best for you.

Here are questions we might ask about Doing and Being in our everyday lives: How can we develop abilities with each? How do you learn to move from one to the other? How do we learn to notice when we are overbalanced toward one or the other? In other words, how can we use Being and Doing to help us live happier and healthier ways? Think of it this way. We can get out of balance within each of the three levels: the body, the mind, and the spirit. We can also get out of balance by over- or under-emphasizing one of these three at the expense of the other two. That is, ideally, we need to be balanced between the levels and also within the levels.

First, let's look at imbalance and balance within each level.

On the body level, think of Doing as heavy exercise like body building, weightlifting, or running. Here your energy is focused on a task, it's being expended in a heavy way. In contrast, think of Being as attending to the body through activities such as stretching or Hatha yoga. Here your energy is focused inward as you observe the feel of your muscles, follow your breath, and try to guide the body toward flexibility.

Obviously, both of these approaches are beneficial. What's important is not to overdo one at the expense of the other. If you overdo the weightlifting, you can hurt yourself. If all you do is stretch, you won't have enough strength. It's best to stretch before a hard run and build strength as well as to stretch for flexibility.

One of my favorite examples is about a group of high school football players. They were at a camp where their unit leader was a six-foot, two-hundred-and-fifty-pound former pro football player. They did plenty of strength training, but he also had them out every morning learning dance exercises and stretching taught by a ballet instructor. Conversely, yoga enthusiasts and dancers can exercise for strength, often through practices or postures that have them holding their body weight. Holding plank position for several minutes will certainly strengthen plenty of muscles.

The balance will be different for different people. Some will be drawn toward Doing, like strength training, while others will naturally incline toward Being, like stretching. We all need some of each, but the proportions will be different for each individual. Take time to think about how you attend to your body. Are you happiest pushing yourself to a marathon run, or do you prefer a gentle stroll? Do you prefer mild Hatha yoga or fierce versions of Ashtanga? Then think about whether you have a reasonable balance for yourself. If so, great. If not, maybe build in more of the approach that feels less natural at first.

Here's an exercise to try:

After a vigorous workout, just stand and let your body move itself. Watch and see how the energy moves you. This would be a way of Being after the Doing of the form. Another exercise would be to follow a hard run with a little dance. Get a DVD of a dance you might like or put on some music and do a dance you know. After five to ten minutes of this, stand still, play music or DVD, and let your body move by itself. This would be an example of going from a vigorous Doing to a more flowing Being. You can also try these experiments in the opposite direction.

Now let's look at the level of mind. In this category, I include both intellect and emotion. I realize that it's a matter of current dispute and fascinating research to consider the relation of these two [see Damasio, for example], but for our purposes, let's talk on a rather common-sense level.

Of course, we all have both intellect and emotion. As was the case on the body level, most of us are inclined more toward one or the other. Take music, for example. Someone who's tilted toward Doing is likely to be very intellectual and to focus intently on being technically perfect. Overbalancing in this direction will lead to music that may be technically great and intellectually interesting but that won't have passion, won't connect with the audience except as intellectual exercise. Someone who's heavily into emotion may have power but also may have trouble conveying a form or a meaning, and his or her music will be all over the place. One of the reasons the music of composers like Bach, Mozart, Beethoven, and Verdi endures is that their work has extraordinary structure combined with extraordinary passion.

It's no accident that Mozart's music is sometimes used to aid healing, for example, being played during acupuncture sessions.

Another example of someone who overbalances toward Doing on the mind level is the religious scholar who hyperfocuses, can recite holy text at length and analyze it rigorously, but who stays coldly intellectual. Such a scholar may be brilliant but is not likely to get close to God. The impressive but coldly intellectual Casaubon from George Eliot's *Middlemarch* is a good example of the icily studious man.

On the other hand, someone who has only an emotional connection to a text can't explain what the beauty is, can't communicate to others or even to himself. He may be wrapped in emotional ecstasy, but that alone is ultimately egotistical and can lead to blind fanaticism. Such people may have an explosive temper, may be drama queens, may be scattered and all over the place.

Again, most of us naturally lean one way or the other but try to be aware and to work to balance your tendencies.

Here are exercises to try on the mind level:

If you tend to analyze everything, go to a beach or to the woods. Just sit there and let your mind expand. Ask yourself, "What do you feel?"

When you have to make a decision, and you notice that you've listed every pro and con, pause and try to see what your gut reaction is. Try to feel what your body is telling you. When you look at the cons, does your stomach tighten up? When you look at the pros, do your shoulders hunch? Observing such responses is valuable for decision-making, just as rational analysis is. In fact, some current brain research suggests that our brains make our decisions before we're even aware that they have done so. Tuning into bodily reactions, Being with them, can help us see what's happening on the preconscious level.

Another way to access the Being part of yourself is to do some spontaneous writing. Sit in a comfortable position and observe your breathing for a few minutes. Don't do anything or try to change anything; simply be aware of the breath coming in and going out. Wait until your mind calms down. Then take a pad of paper and pen or pencil; just sit there and let yourself write whatever comes out.

If your quick and customary response is emotional, sometimes try to Do, to look at what's going on and articulate it. Notice a time when you get worked up about something and pause, breathe deeply; then see what's going on and lay out the issues. Or when you're in a heavy emotional state, try to Do something. Take a walk, sing a song, or draw a picture. This will serve to focus your mind (a Doing). Then sit down and see how different you are.

Okay, we've looked at the body and the mind levels. Finally, let's look at spirit. I think of spirit as an essence within us which connects to the energy of the Universe. Some people pray to God, some go into trance states, some meditate, and some connect through action. Whatever you do to connect to some force without or within yourself, balance is important here too.

Consider, for example, two different types of meditation: Doing and Being. Doing is active, such as focusing on a mantra or visualizing energy going up and down in your body. Being is when you just sit, breathe, relax, and observe which way the energy moves.

Each kind of meditation balances the other. For example, just Being with your breath, noticing the in and out of your breathing, would balance the strong mental focus of visualizing or wrestling with a koan. If you repeatedly do only one kind or the other, you're limiting yourself, just like weightlifting without stretching.

Here's an exercise for the spirit level:

First try Doing, using focus and direction. Visualize yourself in your favorite place. This place can be real or imaginary; it doesn't matter. Notice the sights, sounds, smells, and the energy of the place. Feel the air. Feel the sun on your body or the cool of shade and darkness. Stay there for a while. Notice the energy it takes to stay there, the focus that is needed.

Now come back to the present. Just sit in a comfortable position. Follow your breathing in and out. Just Be. Do you notice the calmness? The ease in just being there? The two types of connecting to spirit are different. Can you feel that? One is not better than the other. They just produce different results. They balance each other.

As we become more aware of Doing and Being modes on each level, and as we become aware of our tendencies and work to balance them, we can become skillful. We can notice what a situation calls for, notice when we're out of balance, and call on Being or Doing as needed.

Now let's look at the need for balance among the three levels.

A person who is too heavy on the body will tend not to think clearly enough (too little mind) and will not have a way to connect to the Universe (too little spirit). Think of figures such as Hercules or Samson, men who got into big trouble because they focused on developing and using their bodies so much that they often didn't see mistakes, threats, or temptations. A more modern example would be an athlete who's so focused on physical achievement that he doesn't care if he shortens his life by taking steroids. Doing so may bring a high salary in professional sports, but it doesn't help one live one's life in a way that has much meaning intellectually, emotionally, or spiritually.

Someone who hyperfocuses on the mind might neglect the body, its needs or safety. Think of intellectuals who are physically weak, or who, as a Harvard alumna observed, may "understand quantum physics but don't know how to tie their shoes." The absent-minded intellectual who falls into a pit because he's thinking so hard is a stock character going back to Chaucer. Or consider the story of a brilliant nineteenth-century Russian scholar of the Talmud, a man who was so wrapped up in his ideas that he forgot that Jews who were out of doors on Easter were likely to be murdered by Cossacks. All the other Jews stayed indoors on that day, but he forgot and wandered down the street because he was thinking so hard, and was killed. All those hours of study, all the work of those who supported him so he could study, were wasted.

Is it possible to be too much in the spirit? Yes indeed. Someone who's always off in a trance state isn't connected to ordinary reality and can cause problems for self and others. A Kundalini master became so sensitive that he couldn't function, and his wife had to do everything for him, even reminding him to eat and bathe. To counterbalance such excess of the spiritual, some medieval monasteries prudently said, "no work, no food." *Ora et labora*: work and prayer. A friend told my teacher of a woman who had vivid visions, who took long shamanic journeys, and who could see the past lives of herself and others. My teacher replied, "Everyone can have visions, but can she heal?" Her point was that the mystic who is always unconnected to ordinary life is egotistical, that one who doesn't connect to anything in the ordinary world is not of service to anyone.

Ezekiel told of his visions so people could get a glimpse of the holy, Mother Teresa prayed to enable her to help the poor. The Dalai Lama takes what he gains from deep meditation to bring others toward happiness. My ideal is to be of service. Others can do what they want, go after only their own salvation, but I'd rather use spirit to help people, and that means interweaving it with body

Ho'o Pono Pono

In addition to working on balancing Being and Doing, I was learning to use a system called Ho'o Pono Pono. There I discovered a way of not judging myself for having tendencies toward violence. Instead of being afraid or clamping down on myself when I was angry and felt like lashing out, I learned that what I needed to do was feel compassion toward myself.

First, a little background on Ho'o Pono Pono. It's a Hawaiian shamanic system that focuses on mediation and reconciliation. It was originally used between groups to mediate disputes and now is used to mediate disputes within oneself. It's similar to Buddhist Metta meditation and Tonglen meditation, in that it means to cultivate loving energy and compassion. The difference is that in Ho'o Pono Pono you don't send energy out, you focus it inward. The compassion is for yourself.

I've adapted the traditional system in ways that seem to be most helpful for me and for the people I work with. The traditional version is based on the belief that you create everything in the world that you encounter. For example, if you have trouble with someone, you helped create that trouble, and by changing yourself, you can help heal the trouble or at least shift your response to it. If you are interested in the Hawaiian shamanic system, there's a very accessible account in *Zero Limits* by Joe Vitale and Dr. Ihaleakala Hew Len.

My understanding is that you are responsible for everything you feel. So, if you're having a problem, it's your problem, not the other person's. Sure, if someone comes in to me and is angry, I can see that it's his anger, not something I've created. Nonetheless, often one person's energy, emotion, or state can affect others. In the old days, someone else's anger could make me angry or afraid. Now, as soon as someone's energy impinges on my energetic sphere, I can feel it and know I need to clean it, to let go of that energy.

Again, the image that seems to fit is that of a mirror that can gather dust. In this case, the dust that accumulates is the emotions of others. If I don't keep cleaning that mirror, if the dust of others' emotions that affect me builds up, the mirror won't reflect anymore, it can't function as a helpful mirror. So, I can't just blame the other person for how I'm reacting; I'm responsible for keeping myself in the state I want to be in.

It's not that we don't want to be helpful and compassionate. It's that we need to be clear on what is ours and what is theirs. Then, in fact, when we are clear, when we protect ourselves, we can be most helpful to others. How do we do this? How do we clean the mirror? How do we keep ourselves from letting the emotions of others control the way we feel and function?

We visualize or feel the energy that's coming to us. When someone sends anger to me, I notice myself getting angry back. When someone tries to lure me to charge in and help but doing so would not help her and might drain me, I feel an impulse to action. I need to see what is happening. My process is to look at what's happening. Others, people who react emotionally first, who sense what's going on through their feelings, might become aware of and sense the emotions impinging and building.

My reaction—be it anger, fear, or temptation—is mine and it's up to me to let it go. To let it go, I need to release my attachment to the energy that has come into me. When I say I'm attached, I mean I stay connected to the feeling the other person has elicited, I keep feeling the anger or whatever. The way to release this attachment, this jump to anger or to temptation, is to love the part of myself that is being angry or being tempted.

Further, if we have a reaction to something, especially a powerful reaction, it can mean there's something in our past that needs to be healed. By sending love to that past hurt, that past suffering self, we can release the way we're still feeling that old response, release the way we're attached in the present to the old emotional response that has been evoked.

The key is that we cannot change the past, but we can change our attachment to the past. We cannot change the way our father treated us or our reaction when we were small. But we can change the way we keep reacting the same way in similar situations. To do this, we can go back to that image of ourselves as little and send love to our hurt in that situation. We can also journey back to past lives that included similar situations. We do seem to keep being reborn with the same lessons to learn until we find a way to resolve them. The next chapter will give an expanded example of how this works.

Here I'll just say that, following the teaching of Ho'o Pono Pono, when I feel anger or confusion or any other kind of pain, I say to it, "I love you." That may sound simplistic, but with practice it works. If someone is cruel, I feel the hurt in myself and right away try to be fully aware of it. Then I stop, I don't react, I look at the hurt, and say, "I love you" to myself feeling that hurt, whether it's myself in the present situation, an evocation of old hurt from childhood, or even hurt that is deep because it's been repeated in successive lives.

At this point, you may think that this system resembles the approach of psychotherapy, finding the sources of old pain and thus getting free of them. I see it differently because regular psychotherapy hopes that if you can understand the past, you can release it. Maybe that happens for some people, but it's not my experience with myself or the people I work with. Ho'o Pono Pono also differs from approaches that say to love your inner child because it works with an entire life's worth of attachments. It's not enough to see and identify or love the inner child. Furthermore, what's hurting may not be the child. You need to go further and deeper than that.

Metta, loving kindness, and religious love, like the Christian ideal of loving your neighbor and your enemy, may make a focus on loving the self seem too restricted, even selfish or narcissistic. Loving kindness is a beautiful practice, and there are people for whom it works beautifully. For me, it just isn't strong enough; it's just not my way or my practice. My way is an alternative; I'm not trying to claim it's better.

My experience is that focusing on loving others sends one's energy out, and then the energy tends to disperse, not be powerful. Also, you have no control over the other; you do have control over yourself, and if you can heal the microcosm, the internal, the energy will radiate out and can help heal the macrocosm, the other. If you're not clear within, trying to heal others can become egotistical.

Jesus and Buddha weren't just lovey-dovey, nor was Mother Teresa. They were strong, tough people who became sure of themselves after doing much soul searching and coming to terms with who they were. The Japanese god of compassion is symbolized as a fierce warrior with a two-edged sword over his head. It can cut both ways. It has to go in and out.

Philosophers have wrestled with the question of how it is possible to love someone whom you hate. I think that if you hate someone, sending love isn't going to work. Kant, the great German philosopher, argued that love in such cases is not an emotion but a practical duty. That interpretation can be helpful as an ethical guideline, but it doesn't deal with what hate does to you. So, the answer is to realize that hate is within you, and therefore the solution is to love that part of you that is hating in both the present and the past. Once you've released your attachment to your feeling of hate, then there may be the possibility of compassion for the person whom you've hated.

If you would like to try Ho'o Pono Pono, here are a couple of possible approaches. One is for everyday use, for times when a negative emotion pops up, and the other is for cultivating Ho'o Pono Pono through practice in order to loosen attachments in the long term.

What I mean by a "negative emotion" is simply one that is harmful to us, that hurts, that knocks us off balance, that keeps us from Being and Doing in ways that help us. Such emotions may be obvious like anger, fear, or self-criticism when used in ways that hinder us. I say "when used in ways that hinder us" because sometimes these emotions can be helpful, as when righteous anger spurs us to counter injustice, or when self-criticism allows us to identify and then improve a weakness. Even emotions that we usually think of as positive, like pity or benevolence, can be used harmfully, for example, to keep us from attending to what we or others may most need. As the saying goes, giving a man a fish is less beneficial than helping him learn to fish. Are we trying to make ourselves feel good or to help him? We need to be discerning and honest about whether an emotion is harmful or not.

First, let's look at what I call everyday Ho'o Pono Pono. Here I'm talking about noticing, catching, and shifting negative emotions when they arises. Since emotions can be strong but also a little tricky, the first step is feeling the emotion. The second is awareness of the emotion, itself. What are you feeling? It can help to name it. Sometimes it will be obvious what the emotion is: "I'm so angry I want to punch that guy in the nose." Sometimes it's more subtle; often under anger lies fear or hurt. Sometimes it helps us to notice what's going on in our bodies. "My stomach is clenching up; usually this means I'm feeling afraid." Where in your body do you feel hard emotions? Stomach? Head? Shoulders? At this point, don't judge the emotion or try to get rid of it. Just observe.

The third step is to become aware of whether this emotion is one that you need or one that you want to let go of. This can take keen awareness. Is understanding someone who has hurt us—usually a good thing—freely leading to forgiveness or is it keeping us from feeling some anger and resentment that lie below the surface?

Once we're aware that what we're feeling is a negative emotion, the next question is whether we're attached to it. We may just feel something and then the feeling passes. Meditators talk of an emotion as being like a cloud that passes through the sky. We feel it, notice it, and watch it move on. We can, however, get attached to emotions, including those that hinder us. By "attached" I mean that the emotion stays with us, almost as if we were tethered to it or as if it had grown roots in our hearts (or wherever).

When we're angry, for example, we tend to think of all the things that so and so did to make us angry, we repeatedly tell our friends of our grievances, and then we get even angrier. Or we may be afraid and keep thinking of the terrible things that may happen to us. Most of us know this experience, one that can keep us awake in the middle of the night. Round and round our minds go, and we sink deeper into the emotion. Whenever we attach to an emotion, we feed it.

Or to shift the metaphor, a negative emotion acts like a dam in a river. We can keep piling up against it, or we can figure out a way to flow around it. Ho'o Pono Pono can help us flow around it, can help us when we're tied to a negative emotion.

When you've followed the steps above and believe you're sticking with a negative emotion, simply say to yourself, "I love you. I'm sorry. Please forgive me. Thank you."

Just saying these words may sound artificial and mechanical, but it can help. I've seen it help many of the people I work with. What we're doing here is trying to interrupt a pattern. We're trying to break a cycle by distracting the mind from the negative feeling or thoughts. It's not denial but rather using the way the mind works. For all its complexity, the mind tends to focus on one thing at a time (multi-tasking involves rapid switching more than simultaneity). If we can get the mind focused on a positive saying, on being gentle with itself, it can't simultaneously be talking negative chatter to itself. We're replacing a negative thought or feeling with a positive one. That's why affirmations work for some people and why Koans can help distract the mind from ordinary chatter.

Such use of Ho'o Pono Pono can help when we're caught by a negative emotion in an everyday kind of way. Longer term, we need what I call "Practice Ho'o Pono Pono." I use this phrase because we can go beyond distracting ourselves to actually healing what causes the attachments. If we always get angry when someone threatens us, this is a repeating pattern, a long-term reflex reaction, an attachment to anger. Others may habitually respond to threat by appeasing or retreating. After all, we could respond to the threat by ignoring it, or by assessing it and acting pragmatically, or by meeting it with competitive glee.

Changing such patterns requires regular practice, not just first aid.

Once you've identified a pattern of negative emotion, it's time to set about healing whatever caused it. Every day try to picture a time in your life that was traumatic, a time in which you strongly experienced the emotion you want to let go of. See yourself clearly: How old were you? What was happening? Where were you? Who else was there?

Then interact with yourself in the vision. Embrace that person, console him or her, be compassionate and caring for yourself as you are in the vision, just as if you were holding a little baby that was crying. Keep doing this until the vision changes into one that is positive or until another vision of yourself with that powerful emotion comes up. If another vision of yourself with that powerful feeling does arise, just do the same thing. You may need to sit with this practice for many days. Doesn't matter; just keep working with it. It doesn't matter which episode in your life you envision. Just keep sending love to that part of yourself which is in pain. Here, you're sending the love inward, not outward.

Say, for example, you see yourself as a little boy being yelled at by a hypercritical father. You're not sending love to the father (though later you may forgive him or feel compassion for him); you're sending love to that part of you that was injured by your father. Do so by saying, "I love you" over and over to yourself as the child who was yelled at. Hold him in your heart and give him compassion. You can also say, "I'm sorry, please forgive me" to the little boy.

Sometimes when you're having the vision, a different word or phrase will come to you. If this happens, use that word or phrase instead of "I love you." It doesn't have to make sense; it will be a healing mantra.

As you continue to practice, the scene may get fuzzy and eventually dissolve or disappear. As this happens, emotional healing is occurring, and you will gradually find that the intensity and duration of the negative emotion will cease.

The example in the next chapter will tell the story of someone whose fear kept her from a balanced response to a difficult situation. Though very skeptical at first, being a trained analytical thinker, she found that using Ho'o Pono Pono, learning to feel compassion for herself, helped loosen the fears tenaciously rooted in her past.

Ariel

This chapter and the next look at two cases where the biggest obstacle to balance is fear. In the first, we'll look at how using love, through Ho'o Pono Pono, will help someone who has a hard time with fear.

It may seem that the opposite of love is hate or perhaps anger, but often what keeps us from love is actually fear. Anger or hate may be present, but they may be a defense against a fear that lies behind them. Think about the times when a person lashes out because he's afraid. Thus fear of being hurt can keep us from loving others. It can also keep us from loving ourselves. In fact, what we need to do in order to overcome fear is to love the part of ourselves, which is fearful.

Not surprisingly, given what I've been saying about balance, the fear in the case of Ariel was intensified by another kind of imbalance. Ariel is a powerful hyperfocuser who uses her intellect to solve problems. This is her way of Doing: clear sharp focus on a problem, weighing of pros and cons, testing out alternative solutions. She needed to balance this Doing with Being. Specifically, what she needed was to feel compassion (a kind of Being) for her fearful self in addition to her usual Doing method of analyzing what was causing the fear. As she did so, she lessened her fear.

When Ariel's mother died a few months ago, Ariel became the executrix of her mother's estate. Though she was saddened by her loss and knew that dealing with estates can be complicated and time consuming, she thought that she'd get through the difficulties by figuring out what needed to be done and then doing it.

Life wasn't so simple. When she came into the office, she was looking tense and shaky.

When I asked how she was doing, she answered, "Not so hot. My siblings are giving me a hard time about my mother's estate. I know that money can cause trouble in families, but I feel emotionally battered by their pressure and am also, and I assume therefore, having serious stomach trouble to boot. All my work with meditation, yoga, rational philosophy hasn't been much help, so I'm feeling like sort of a jerk too."

I pointed out that she'd long had trouble dealing with difficult emotions. "Now we have to figure out why." I knew her family background, so it wasn't too hard to figure out where to start.

Ariel's mother was powerful—very smart, very driven to create a life better than she'd had in a poor immigrant family, focused on helping her husband build his law practice.

As Ariel describes her, "she was so focused on keeping things under control that when we kids caused any ripples, she would turn on us with anger, powerful, flaming anger. My father, also very smart, was a superb lawyer, beloved by his clients, devoted to his practice, but reluctant to deal with the messiness of family dynamics. Whenever things got uncomfortable, he'd go to the office or to his workshop and let my mother deal with whatever was going on.

"The result was that my siblings and I were given an economically comfortable home and excellent educations, praised when we did well academically and intellectually, and left to cope with emotions on our own. Not surprisingly, I became fearful of emotions; I saw my brother having terrible fights with my mother when he tried to question or rebel; I saw a younger sister scorned when she whined because she craved attention and needed love. The logical inference was that feelings were scary, that to express or even have strong feelings was just asking for trouble. Strong feelings just scared the hell out of me even though I was actually pretty passionate myself. As a colleague once said of herself, 'I metaphorically cut my throat, cut off any connection between brain and heart.'

"I hid my own desire for passion because I sure wasn't going to make myself vulnerable to the unpredictable reactions of my family. It would be too easy to get laughed at or ignored or attacked. So, I learned to act rational or to disappear when feelings ran high. My way of coping when I either got upset or saw trouble in the family, was to hide from my fear—physically hide by going into the woods or holing up in my room, emotionally hide by not letting myself even feel my feelings, and intellectually and spiritually hide by looking to books and abstract thought. My favorite refuge was reading a book while up in a tree."

"What happened," I said in response to Ariel's explanation, "was that you built a box around yourself to protect yourself from frightening emotions. Since you're a strong seer and hyperfocuser, and since you were encouraged to develop your intellectual gifts, you first try to analyze a situation and figure out a rational way to proceed. If that doesn't work or if the emotions are too strong and distressing, you feel deep fear. That's what happened when you felt as if your siblings were attacking you. You care about them and want a close relationship, so to feel attacked by them and to see no way to resolve the problem made you panic.

"The walls of the box are constructed by fear. We all have parameters we operate in, those we are comfortable with. I'm asking you to take away the walls of the box, which are limiting, restricting. Yes, the walls are based on experience and have protected you. You learned very young that when your emotions (or those of others) got scary, it was safest to suppress your feelings, to analyze the situation rationally, or to hide. These methods were clever and protected you as a youngster, but now they aren't working, and that scares the dickens out of you. It's fear that makes you stay within these ways of dealing with emotions, which scare you. Fear boxes you in and keeps you from trying other kinds of responses. But limiting yourself to either analysis or withdrawal boxes you in, keeps you from other possible ways of responding.

"We need to help you find another way to deal with threatening emotions. But we can't just assault the walls; that would be too scary. If we don't have our familiar defenses against what scares us, we feel as if nothing's anchored, we panic, flail, strike out."

I gave her a physical example: once a couple vacationed on a lovely island in the Caribbean. The accommodation was right on the beach, where they could see and hear the waves and feel the warmth and the breeze. The problem was that the hut had no walls. The couple flipped out because they didn't feel safe. Or here's another: a man grew up in Co-op City, an area of the Bronx that has about twenty to forty thousand people living there. One apartment block after another, its own schools, post office, etc. This guy received a promotion at work and moved from Co-op City to Andover, MA, a Boston suburb with large homes, big green lawns, old trees, and a small, uncrowded shopping center.

He couldn't stand it and moved back to the Bronx with its noise, lights, and dense population. That was his familiar box.

"If you can dissolve the fear that keeps you restricted," I told her, "You will feel more expansive, freer, more able to keep balance in difficult situations."

"Fine," she said, "how do I do this? Lord knows I've tried the usual routes, therapy, meditation, reading, thinking, and self-discipline to do what I find hard. They've all helped, but I still have trouble with the fear of being attacked and of people abandoning me."

I laughed. "You're going to be tough because of your strengths. We use our strengths to preserve what makes us feel safe. A feeling person will try to love the attacker into abandoning the fight; a thinker will put her energy into figuring things out intellectually. In your case, as a seer and hyperfocuser who's been trained to use intellect, you're going to use those to hold feelings in check. The stronger the mind, the stronger the walls of the box. A powerful intellect will hold the emotions back so there's no leakage. Someone with a less powerful mind won't be able to control their emotions so well and thus will become more used to feeling them. You're able to focus your mind on whatever you want rather than feel the emotions."

"Ah, so that's why ever since I could read, my reaction to stress has been to go away and read a book. So now what do I do?"

"Well, usually, at first, we can't see what really caused the problem we're facing; we just see what's right on the surface and know that there's a lot of emotion around this issue. As soon as you feel fear or edgy, given your nature and training, you may try to figure out why, but what I'm suggesting is that you do not immediately try to analyze why you panic when someone attacks you. As soon as you feel the fear, just say, 'I love you.'"

"Huh? Just saying words? That's not going to do it."

"What we're trying to do is replace a negative, painful emotion with a positive one. Remember that emotions exist just in our consciousness. Though they certainly can feel strong and real, they exist only in our minds. They can come and go, passing through our minds the way a cloud passes through the sky. Now, if you attach to the fear, or any other painful emotion, it will stay with you. But if you can focus on a positive feeling, the negative one will move on across the sky. We want to replace the negative one with a positive one."

"That's all fine in theory, John, but just saying 'I love you' to myself isn't really going to make me stop being afraid. I'll know I'm just saying that and will believe the fear is still strong and present underneath all the new age palaver."

"It goes deeper than that. I'm not just talking about so-called affirmations, which may work for some who are ready but not for hard cases like you."

Ariel got it that I was letting her know that I was going to stick with her as she went through the process. She also got that I was being funny and paying her a backhanded compliment at the same time as I was defining why the problem was so recalcitrant. Just being seen is comforting.

"Let's break the process into steps and go a little deeper. First, when you feel fear or panic, stop whatever you're doing and name it. Say, 'I am feeling fear.'

"Then ask yourself, 'What is the fear?' For example, 'I'm afraid my brother and sister won't love me and I'm all alone.'

"Third step is to ask, 'Is this fear mine or not mine?' Sometimes, a sensitive person will feel someone else's emotions. Maybe what's going on is the other person's problem; maybe he is afraid of something, and I've picked up the feeling and think I have to fix it. If the feeling really isn't mine, then it isn't my problem, and I can let it go or try to be helpful in an objective if sympathetic way.

"Fourth, if it is your feeling, ask, 'Is it true?' Perhaps, your siblings really are loving or are merely trying to have some input, and you're just having a panic attack. If that's the case, you can tell yourself that your fear is unrealistic; they do love you.

"If the feeling is true, if they really are attacking and this reveals that you can't count on them to care for you, and that you really are alone, see whether you can get a vision of what it looks like to be alone. What image comes to your mind of yourself alone? Is it of yourself after your husband died? Is it of a little girl sitting by herself in a field? Is it of a little girl terrified because her parents are angry with each other? These images will recur and will go farther and farther back in your life. Send love to each one.

"Finally, go back until you get to what I call 'the gatekeeper.' This will probably be the youngest memory of being alone. She is the gatekeeper of that emotion, of that side of the box. Keep sending love to her. Whenever you feel the fear of being attacked or being alone, skip the other steps and go back to the gate keeper.

"Such images pop up all the time."

Here, to persuade Ariel that she wasn't weird or inadequate, I gave her an example from my own life.

"I had an image of a time I was in nursery school. My mother took me to another house for a play date. She left me with a mother that I knew and went off on an errand. The kids I was with wanted to go down the street to play with some other kids. (That was considered safe back then.) I went with them past a couple of houses, and then we went down a driveway beside a big yellow house and saw the other kids playing in the back yard. I freaked, ran back to the first house, and stayed there sitting on the steps until my mother came back and picked me up.

"There are layers to this memory image. I felt abandoned by my mother, and this built on a past life experience of being a teenager in a concentration camp, without anyone I knew. As I sat with this image and simply kept looking at it, I became the little person, walked to the second house, and felt that there was something wrong with it. I went down the driveway and saw a spirit in the backyard. As my adult self, I said to the little boy who was me, 'I love you,' because he needed to be healed from his terror. I said to the spirit, 'It's all over, there's nothing for you here, I love you too.'

"Over time, as I went back to this scene again and again, the vision, instead of being crystal clear got foggy around the edges, like an impressionist painting. Then it became only light, very beautiful, then it faded. Now when I go back, the little boy isn't there anymore. I can see the place and it's just a place with light. No emotion, no spirits, no attachment. Sometimes when I go back, the place isn't even there anymore.

"Keep going back to whatever needs to be released."

Ariel looked away. She explained, "While you were telling your story, I had a vision of my own, perhaps the first memory I have of being terrified. I was about three or four. My mother had dressed me up to take me with her and her sister, my beloved Aunt Sarah, for an excursion to Wellesley, an upscale town where they loved to browse and shop. This would be a rare treat, to end with a stop at a special hot fudge sundae shop. They usually went by themselves, so to be allowed to go with them was huge.

"My mother dressed me in a special outfit, a little white dress with apples on it, red and orange, and three narrow lines of red ribbon just above the waist. Even wearing a dress was special because I was usually in overalls since I tended to play rough in the fields and trees. She told me to go out and play until they were ready to leave.

"Predictably enough, I went out to the field behind our house and in playing there tore the dress on a fallen tree branch. My mother was furious. She put me down hard into my crib or bed and said I couldn't go to Wellesley with them. She looked like a demon queen, the evil queen in Snow White, raging at me in fury. Sweet Aunt Sarah looked sad and loving but couldn't do anything to intervene. I was flat out terrified. Sobbing, crying out in fear."

I let there be a little silence while the vivid image set. Then I told Ariel to talk with the little girl, to let her know that the grown-up Ariel was there. I said to have a conversation with little Ariel, to tell her you love her.

"Oh, rats, John, there it is again, just saying the words. That doesn't seem to work for me. In the past I've tried having conversations with various images I've gotten in visions, but doing so never led to any response or anything else."

I needed to give Ariel a way to feel the love. Just seeing and using words wasn't going to change anything because that's the way she always dealt with things, and it wasn't going to work here to change her fear. She needed to feel. Again, balance was needed.

I tried to connect her with her own experience of love. "It's like holding a puppy or like when you held your grandchildren as babies. Just cradle the little girl like that, and keep saying 'I love you.' This way, your focus will be on the love not the fear. Eventually the feeling of love will come, and you will feel a connection to the little girl. Your heart will open, and you'll go to a space of love. Then the energy rushes in, the light rushes in.

"Try to feel the love for her, and only then hyperfocus a little. People who hyperfocus tend to hyperfocus first then try to feel love. But you can't make love happen just through discipline (though of course discipline's a fine thing).

"Think back to how Carin told us she helped the dragonfly who was drowning in her mug of tea. After gently lifting it out and placing it on the deck railing, first she loved the dragonfly, brought it in the loving space of her heart; then she focused. At that point, and not before, she looked at the end of the dragonfly's tail; it was unmoving instead of flickering up and down as such tails normally do. As she watched, the tail started to move. She spoke to the body, asking it to warm. Then she asked the delicately veined wings to dry and start to flutter, and they did. She focused on the little being's eyes and head, which then started to move back and forth. Finally, she told it that she hoped it would live and fly, and it lifted off from the railing and flew to the woods beyond her deck.

"First, she loved, was in a place of Being, letting love flow through her. Then she focused.

"Doing takes a lot of one's own energy to hyperfocus and maintain the hyperfocus. Being is a letting go of one's own energy. The energy is supplied and rushes in. The experience of how you get to feeling the energy of the Universe, letting it move you, colors your expression of that energy."

A couple of weeks later, when Ariel and I met again, she looked more settled and steady. Not out of the woods yet but moving. I asked her to tell me how things had gone.

She said, "I tried to go back to the scene of the gatekeeper, me as a little girl in an apple-printed dress, terrified as my mother the demon queen yells at me furiously. I tell the little girl with black ringlets and rounded arms that I love her and will protect her from the rage blasting down at her. Strangely, I also feel a little sorry for my mother who needs to feel such rage and lash out so ferociously, and for my loving Aunt Sarah, who feels such regret and guilt that she can't intervene and soften the fury landing on me. I reach down to pick the little girl up, and she nestles against me and puts her arms around my neck. She becomes less distinct, seems to be merging into me.

"As I've gone back to this time and place repeatedly, she's become less clear, almost a blurred space, tan and without features; my mother and aunt have been receding too, becoming more distant and fainter."

Ariel has obviously been working hard to connect with past experiences of fear, for she went on to another scene, whether an experience from a past life or an imaging of present feelings, I don't know.

"Another scene that I have travelled to," she said, "is one that has popped up in meditation many times over the years, but I've never known what to make of it except to connect it with my present feelings of abandonment. The scene is a mid-western prairie, flat, gray in dim light. There's a horse-drawn wagon in front of a red setting sun. Sitting in the driver's seat is a stern-faced man, dressed in a nineteenth century dark gray suit and wide-brimmed dark gray hat. He's turned to look down at a woman and child. He's leaving them and is unbending in his decision, impervious to their hurt, anger, abandonment.

"The mother is stunned, standing stiff and stoic. The little girl, maybe six or so, holds her hand, not understanding but frightened that something terrible is going on between her parents. When I went to the scene recently, the little girl turned toward me and I saw that under her bonnet, she had the head and face of a gray wolf. She had turned feral.

"On repeated journeys there, I stroke the little girl's head, tell her she's safe now, keep stroking her head, murmuring as to a frightened animal, not pushing or getting closer than she'll allow. Recently, the wolf head has been flickering in alternation with a child's face, oval and pale with light brown hair.

"I've also seen her and her mother in a small room with brown walls and a fire in a fireplace. Outside a window behind the mother's chair is a cold winter night, with the snow gray in the dusk and tree limbs stretched out bare, black, gnarled; the little girl is a human child sitting at her mother's feet, holding the hem of her skirt. I'm glad that they're sheltered. I feel that they will survive."

All Ariel's work seemed to be opening up access to layers of feelings. She'd connected with her own childhood and a past life. She also started dreaming vividly. You can go with Freud's idea that dreams are the "royal road to the unconscious" or with Jungian or other interpretations. More important than theoretical analysis for this seer, always a tempting diversion, was her actually feeling the emotions, letting herself feel them and not let fear of them block them.

She recounted a dream. "Last night I had a dream that a gorilla lived in my house. She was scary, big, black-haired, strong, but hadn't done any damage. She wanted to stay with me, so I let her, though fearfully. Later in the dream there also appeared a lioness, sleek, muscled, but quite tame. At one point I got scared and called animal control, and someone came and took the gorilla away, but she climbed out of the back of the open green army truck and came home again, so I let her stay. That part of the dream ended with me seated and each animal lying against me, the lioness on my right, the gorilla on my left, as I stroked their fur. I woke up briefly, then went back to sleep.

"After going back to sleep, I dreamt I was in front of my house standing beside my gorilla and saw two other gorillas walking up the side street toward me. [Ariel has two siblings.] I worried that my gorilla might lose control and walk over to be with them, might be controlled by her gorilla nature, like driven desire to be with one's own kind. But by the time I woke up again, she hadn't gone to them.

"Pretty transparent, eh? In the earlier dream, the lioness and the gorilla are parts of me, parts that I'm afraid of and fear might get out of control – the animal parts, the emotions. In the latter dream, the two gorillas are my siblings, and in this case my gorilla is what I learned in childhood, what was ingrained in our upbringing. I fear I'll go back to be with family even though they are threatening and pull on a part of me that I don't want to let loose."

So what was Ariel learning from all this? She typically met situations by thinking them through, by hyperfocusing on the problem and then trying to figure out how to act. When she couldn't solve a problem or meet a danger by hyperfocusing and thinking, she panicked or withdrew. In the terms of this book, she would Do, and if that didn't work, she'd retreat or flee. Now she was having to learn to Be, in the sense of letting love flow in, and trust what would happen. First Be and then Do. Pretty scary, but she's trying.

I advised her that she needed balance between mind and heart, seeing and feeling. In her case, which is unusual, her feelings as well as her thinking are very strong. The intellect and the emotions are both so strong, she needs to be very aware of what's going on in order to know how to balance them in a given situation. Maybe in one situation, hyperfocusing and figuring out a problem will be the best way to go. Maybe another situation will call for her to stop and Be, to let love come in and only then to focus on analyzing what to do. Maybe she will need to let the sharpness, the seeing, the coldness be there but not on the surface where it can scare others. At this point, she may well need to pause when she feels fear coming up, be aware of it, and then go with love or with seeing, as seems called for. With enough practice, the process will get faster.

During our most recent conversation about the situation with her siblings, Ariel said her difficult sister had weighed in again, pushing her to control, insisting on double-checking what she was doing.

"To be honest," she said, "I felt anger and panic again, just wanted to back away and flee her pressure and my panic. I didn't sleep much that night. But I think that because of the work to Be with the fear and to send love to it, the painful emotions lasted a shorter time than before. I have glimpses of increasing distance from the sister who comes at me so inexorably. There's less desperate need to appease. Though I was always taught that family comes first, I've been able to admit that sometimes I don't even like her very much and that there must be times when she doesn't like me either.

"I have to learn that I don't need to be desperate for an ideal family connection. I can acknowledge her energy, charm, and talent, and have some sense of why she is coming on so strong, why she has such a need to push things. I don't know what our relationship will be in the future, but at least it will be grounded in reality. Whatever happens, I can learn to shift the way I see and respond. What she does is hers."

Vesta

In the last chapter, I talked about someone who needed to deal with fear by learning to use Being as well as Doing. In this chapter, let's look at someone who learned to deal with fear by using Doing as well as Being.

Last week when Vesta came to the office for the small group meeting of her healing circle, she paused at the door and said, "I have a cold. Would you rather I not come in?" Smiling at her typical thoughtfulness, we said, "Certainly not, go away." Taking our meaning aright, she laughed and came in.

She looked tired, her blue eyes heavy and darkened, and as she went across to sit on the couch, her step was heavier than her usual dancer's flow. Her clothing is almost always striking and fun, expressively feminine, whether a scarlet cloak, a spring-green shawl made of hemp, or sparkly shoes. Today, though, she was wearing a heavy, dark red knit sweater and fur-lined boots. Instead of jewelry of polished stones set in silver, she wore a simple ceramic blue cross at her neck and small wooden crosses as earrings.

When her mother started to fail months ago and her father started to have trouble caring for her, Vesta drove them to doctors' appointments, figured out how to help them move to a place where they'd get assistance, and found the best place. She oversees their care with efficiency and kindness. Though the responsibility has been grueling and the situation sad, she handled it with grace.

She also was happy that her parents seemed to appreciate her help and expressed their appreciation more openly and affectionately than they ever had in the past. Today, however, for the first time, she looked weighed down.

She emailed us two weeks before saying that her father had a stroke and was in a rehabilitation hospital. She went right over as soon as she heard what had happened and was now driving back and forth forty-five minutes each way every day. Affected by the stroke, his right side was weak, and he was having trouble framing words though he clearly knew what he wanted to say. He was upset that he was "feeling old" (at eighty-nine) and no longer strong.

After Vesta got settled on the couch, we asked how she was doing. Instead of answering directly, she reported on how her father was doing. She said that he was responding quite well to the treatment and his caregivers were pleased with his progress.

This progress didn't seem to lighten her state though. I was troubled that I couldn't feel her energy, which usually undulated and filled the room with loving power. She's a quintessential feeler, one who often operates in the Being mode. Now she was sunk back so deeply, she seemed withdrawn into grayness. Much more than a cold was weighing her down. Something was making her so vulnerable that she'd gotten the cold.

We asked what was going on. She told us that she made the long drive to see her father every day. One day last week, she was standing near his bed, holding his hand, trying to send him loving energy. Now, you need to understand that Vesta can heal people just by surrounding them with her deeply feminine energy. When she works in her bookstore, people come over and start telling her about their pain. Once when she set up a booth at a health fair, she drew a line of people who wanted her to lay hands on them. She is so loving that she doesn't even need to lay on hands; that's merely a way for people to think there's a mechanism for the warmth and healing they feel with her.

As she held her father's hand, he turned toward her and said, "Vesta."

Then he lashed out and attacked her.

"You're weak, you've always been weak. You have no courage, never did."

She told us, "I just froze. I was terrified." As she recounted the story, she put a hand on her chest and looked stunned, as if someone had just punched her.

Here Vesta had thought things were changing between her and her father, getting more loving. Then—wham—he charged at her. I felt his attack on her as being like a bludgeon, a mace.

"No," she said, "it was more like a nuclear bomb exploding.

"When he attacked, it took me by surprise. I went back to the automatic little girl response: fear. Even saying anything was not an option because I was conditioned to obey, not ask questions. His attack took me right back to that mode.

"I was taking in all that energy. It felt like being beaten up. He was more powerful, stronger, I couldn't do anything. Powerless." Here Vesta fell silent.

In the past I would have just attacked Vesta's father, would have moved without even thinking about it in order to protect her. Now, I've learned to wait until it's an emergency. I paused, looked, realized it was her thing or his thing, not mine to fix. If I just charged to the rescue, Vesta wouldn't have the chance to learn and heal.

After we both held silent, Vesta went on. "Because I've been doing the work with you, I realized what was happening and put up a shield. I made myself just disappear behind it. He continued to berate me, but it was like something that hurts you physically; your body is there, but your mind isn't."

As a psychologist, I recognized this as dissociation, a common trauma response.

Given this reaction and Vesta's earlier connection with her childhood, we had to look carefully not only in the present but also all the way back into the past so we could understand what was going on and find the best way for her to heal and grow strong enough not to be hurt by him.

The first thing I saw was that Vesta had sent so much love to her ailing father, had been so glad to have a loving relationship with him, that he felt beholden to her both for all she did physically to help and, especially, for the emotional support and the bond that was building between them. He had always had to be "the man of the family," in control, taking care of others, telling his wife what to do, assessing his children. Feeling loving toward Vesta and accepting, even needing, her love made him feel weak.

As a result, he lashed out in an old pattern. He reverted to the kind of abuse he'd inflicted on her as a child.

"He'd always told me I was stupid, and I believed him because I wasn't quick with the analytical, logical, math kinds of skills at school. He certainly didn't give me any credit for being quick at reading people but dismissed all that as women's stuff. The fact that I was athletic didn't count because I was a girl. In school I never said anything for fear I'd get the answers wrong, and I never dared speak up at home. I comforted myself with my dolls and animals and just tried to please him and stay out of his way."

I pointed out that he didn't much like or respect women and had treated her mother the same way. Vesta's mother had let him dominate their relationship, always going along with his decisions and never intervening when he was rough on the children. For the first time, Vesta brightened a bit.

"You know, it's funny, his primary care doctor told me that since Dad has been away at the Rehab home, my mother has become more active at their assisted living community. She's joining groups, doing activities, seeming much more with it than she had been while he was in charge."

Vesta sat up a bit on the deep couch and reached for a tissue and a cough drop. There was light around her now.

"My brother was there when Dad attacked me. Afterwards, he said that what Dad had done was horrible. When we were kids, Bill didn't react much, I guess because he was treated differently, being a boy, or maybe he didn't really see what was going on with me. But after we left Dad's room, he kept saying to me, 'That was so horrible. I can't believe he did that to you.'"

I wasn't sure whether the sharpness I felt near Vesta was hers or her father's, but I knew she had to protect herself from him. I told her she needed to deal with what's real.

"You need to deal with the fact that he has attacked you and may well attack again."

"I know," she replied. "I thought that I needed to be like Gandolf, you know, from *Lord of the Rings*. In the scene where he's standing on the bridge that is crumbling, and there's fire all around, and the great evil is coming at him, and he says something like, 'You may not do this.'"

I demurred. "That's the loving way, the way you would instinctively choose, given who you are, an amazingly loving person. But that's not going to work this time; it won't protect you enough. Loving (which I think of as part of the Being mode) won't keep his attacks from devastating you. You need to bring in the Doing.

"The Doing is about protection, it's outer, it's for clearing darkness, separating souls, sending hurtful attackers away. After you act to protect yourself, then you can move to the Being, the inner healing, the uses of love."

"What do I need to do if I can't love him into change and if I can't stop fearing him?"

"You're angry, aren't you, and that makes you uncomfortable."

"Well, yes."

Now Vesta was leaning forward, and her head seemed less heavy. She hadn't needed to blow her nose for the last five minutes.

"What you've got to do is send his anger back to him. It's his. When you feel anger coming up in you, first just notice that you're feeling anger. Then tell yourself that the anger belongs to him. Tell him that you are sending the anger to him, that you don't want it."

I saw her flinch and knew she was worrying about causing damage or pain to him even though he'd attacked her.

"Don't worry," I said, "you won't harm him – I know you'll worry about that – but he's the one whose fury is blazing out and lighting the anger in you. It is in fact his anger, so you're just returning to him what is his, not causing him harm."

Vesta seemed a little unsure about shifting to this new way of protecting herself. She was not to withdraw and hide, nor do what the other person wanted or even needed. She had to realize what her karma was and what was his. Not karma in some metaphysical sense of past life analysis (though I don't rule that out), but in this case karma means what his actions are and what they lead to, and what her actions are and what they lead to. We have to see clearly who's responsible for which actions and what the consequences of those actions are for the person doing them as well as for others.

By the end of our meeting, Vesta still had her cold, but she looked a whole lot better. She was sitting with a sense of resilience and was smiling at our proffered suggestions of what kinds of cough drops worked best. She bent over to gather her things, got up from the couch with a smooth movement, and put on her cloak gracefully. It wouldn't be easy for her, but she understood what she needed to do and would work hard.

I was confident because over the years we've worked together, she has shyly come to believe that she has unique gifts. She lets her energy dance and undulate. She's learned to trust her intuition. She can tell when winter is starting to shift into spring long before the snow is gone, and she deals with disappointment with a calm sense that if something hasn't happened as she'd hoped, that's okay and something else will happen that's right. And not passively—she'll think about and go after what to do next.

I've gotten clearer about something from this session too. Recently, I've been excited about the Being, because it's new to me and a mode that seems to go beyond the Doing, which is the warrior mode I've instinctively reacted with. What I'm learning once again is that the key is to have awareness. Before doing anything, I need to pause and be aware of what is real at the moment, in the specific situation. Then I can perceive what I'm called on to do and respond with either Doing or Being, whichever will be most helpful. It's been a long lesson, but it's coming.

A month later, at our next meeting, on a promising April day, Vesta looked radiant. There was a glow from her, and her energy once again radiated out in dancing light movement. She was wearing a subtly striped spring-green and blue shawl, her sandals were decorated with small smooth pebbles, and her necklace pendant was a small horn-shaped light green stone. The difference in her was partly due to the fact that spring is her season, the emergence of growth and light after the winter. But it was also due to her hard work on changing.

When we asked what had happened, what she had done, Vesta replied, "Even at the time my father attacked me, I knew it was his stuff, but I couldn't stop it or do anything about it. I sensed there might be a start of healing because after attacking me for a long time, he said, 'I've criticized you a lot tonight. I love you, please don't give up on me.' But I also knew I'd suffered from his attack and would probably get sick. As you saw, I've had a terrible cold and laryngitis.

"Still, I also knew I had to find a quiet space and do something."

"Yes," I interjected, "intention is critical. We think, 'Okay this is it, we're going to do it,' and the tension reaches a critical mass."

Vesta nodded and went on. "I had to go back to the childhood me; as an adult I had to go back and love that child. I had a vision in my mind, holding that child with the love and soothing I never had as a kid. As a child I wasn't allowed to show hurt, so as an adult I crave to be held, loved. I had to do that for myself.

"As I sat with the vision of holding myself as a child, the energy and the vision fell away. Sort of like a rock exploding, the energy and the vision fluttered down in little pieces, like when you throw confetti and it falls, flutters down.

"Then I felt lighter, my heart area felt lighter. The first breath after that, I felt as if I could breathe again.

"I felt proud of myself and believed that whatever comes along now, I know how to deal with it. Years ago, I'd call on the archetype of Persephone, the goddess of the underworld, the figure who can lead us into the depths of the psyche. I'd say to her, 'Hold my hand, we're going back now.' I'd literally drop down to the floor, and we'd do the work."

"Now it happens quickly, doesn't it," I noted, "because you've done so much work. It takes a while to learn the process of going deep into ourselves, into our pasts, into other realms, but once you've learned, it happens quickly."

We wanted to know how she was with her father now that she's had this experience.

"Now when I go to see my father, I don't feel him as such a powerful person, and I know he won't be able to hurt me. He hasn't attacked me viciously again, but I paused and am ready for him. It's a warrior thing." Here, Vesta smiled at me, acknowledging what she'd learned about balancing so as to know which mode to use.

"When I go into his room, I'm alert and sense what I need to do to protect myself. If he's calm, fine. If there's any anger in him or in me, I send it to him, not with anger but with neutrality. If I feel anything threatening, I say, 'I'll come back another day.' If he does ever attack hard again, I'll just smile and go off his radar. I think of it as disappearing and not giving him a target. I'm not afraid of him because he can't hurt me in any deep way.

"He's actually become loving with me."

Vesta said all this with a sense of pleasure in having learned how to act as she needed. This loving woman, who can heal by just Being and letting the spirit of the Universe come through her, now also can use Doing when she needs to.

Discipline

In the previous two chapters, I talked about Ariel and Vesta working hard at what they needed to learn to overcome their fear. They needed discipline to keep at it. In a similar way, I've needed discipline both to cope with my fear of acting with destructive violence and to move beyond violent action.

We usually think of discipline as an act of willpower, often suppressing what we don't want to do or feel. I would say to myself, "I will not kill that person attacking me."

Such willpower certainly helped me hold back from seriously harming anyone, but as most of us know, saying, "You shouldn't" often doesn't work well enough. We may resist the piece of cake and later on get miserably cranky at everyone, or we may slip into the kitchen at midnight and eat a pint of ice cream. In my case, as I've said, when I just repressed the aggressive energy, held it in, I would get sick. Nor did I want to take the path of those who restrained themselves and then released their aggressive energy by heading for a bar or drugs or sex.

In this chapter, I'd like to talk about another kind of discipline, a kind that has helped me learn not to repress the aggressive energy but to express it through a form, initially through martial arts. I'd also like to note what I've learned about ways that others use discipline. Perhaps there's something in my experience or that of others which you might recognize or find useful.

Discipline is not an easy subject to talk about, however.

The other day when I came into one of the small healing groups that meet in my office, I said that I'd been thinking about discipline and was convinced discipline is necessary for anyone to get where he or she wants. Even these people, who know me well and are highly motivated to grow, pulled away and didn't want to talk about it. In fact, nearly everyone I talk with on the subject has a similar reaction. When I ask why, they say that they feel as if they're being pressured, that discipline sounds like something difficult, something military, a regimen they'd be forced into.

This reaction may have something to do with my being so definite. After a certain point in working with someone, I tend to say, "Without discipline, you aren't going to get anywhere." The conversation comes to a screeching—or frightened—halt.

The negative reaction may be strong also because discipline comes so easily and naturally to me that it's taken me a while to realize that others don't approach it in the same way. "After all," I think, "why wouldn't you just do what helps you? Why would you eat what harms your wellbeing? Why wouldn't you work at what will give you strength and healing?"

The answers are myriad, of course, ranging from "I don't want to live without the pleasures I'd have to give up" to "I don't know, I just can't seem to make myself do X or Y."

Rather than going through the excuses and trying to reason with them one at a time, first I want to talk about what discipline means to me, and why and how I think it's so important. Then I want to deal with broader questions and talk about ways other people, with other gifts, may see or use discipline.

If it will make the discussion easier, think of the topic not as discipline, but as practice.

Practice alone, though, isn't enough. I learned early on that mere repetition alone wouldn't be enough. I saw some of my high school football teammates practice drills in a rote kind of way. They got stronger, no question, but they didn't become more skillful players. They learned certain moves, but they didn't understand the forms, so they weren't flexible or intelligent players. Nor did they always use their strength in benevolent ways off the field.

Even when I was in my teens, I saw that this kind of practice wouldn't get me where I wanted to go. I came to realize that I needed awareness while I practiced and awareness about my practice. The key elements are practice and awareness. Both are necessary.

Yes, you do need to put in the hours, but practice without awareness is useless. You can do the same push-ups for twenty years, but if you're doing them wrong, you're not getting anywhere. When I drive down the street, I see people running, but rarely do I see anyone running with the correct form. They think they are doing something good for themselves, but they are likely to hurt themselves instead. They need to pay attention to their form, to what is happening in their bodies.

My practice involves a lot of meditating and sitting still, and a lot of movement in martial arts and yoga. Now, I'm not saying that everyone has to have the same practice I do. It doesn't matter what your practice is, so long as you have one. Someone else may be totally different. What practice you're drawn to will depend on what your nature and gifts are. I'm not drawn to music as a discipline because I have no ear. I was originally drawn to fighting because I'm good at it and enjoy it. You may be drawn to computers or to writing or to prayer. It doesn't matter so long as you practice.

Here's an example of my practice: when I learned a new move in Hsing-i, I repeated it a hundred times every day, for a year. I did the move on a flat grassy surface, I practiced it going uphill and downhill, I practiced it on a rocky path, I practiced it in my driveway. A friend said he wanted to learn the move too and practiced with me, but when it started to snow, he went inside while I learned what it felt like to practice the move uphill in the snow and ice. When I came back to my house, he was inside sipping hot coffee in front of the fire. "You're nuts," he said.

Well, maybe so, but this kind of alert repetition helped me become aware of how the move felt from the inside, when it felt right and when it felt off, when it might be effective and when it wouldn't.

Determined practice, with awareness, was necessary.

Why?

The first reason is such practice is necessary for the form to become part of me, necessary for me to gain mastery. Some people think I have unusual gifts, but they don't see how much work has gone into developing those gifts. To use other examples (and I'm not trying to put myself in their category), how many baskets did Larry Bird shoot before he made it to the NBA, and did you know that even once he got there, he showed up at the basketball court before anyone else to practice shooting? What kind of repeated prayer and effort and learning did it take for Jesus to do what he did (remember the night in the Garden of Gethsemane)? The Dalai Lama said that to gain mastery, you have to meditate for 10,000 hours. Jane Goodall may have had an initial passion and talent for observing animals but think of the hours she spent learning to really see and then interact with chimpanzees. Malcolm Gladwell cites examples of people who have such passion for their vocations that they put in about 10,000 hours of practice to become what he calls "outliers." True, Gladwell points out that people like Bill Gates, The Beatles, and great Canadian hockey players have exceptional ability and fortunate opportunities, but he also says that they need the practice and the ability to be aware of and learn from their practice (*Outliers*, pp. 15–55).

Those who have gained mastery may make it look easy, but the process of getting there is definitely not.

You may think, "Well, I'm not Larry Bird or Bill Gates or Buddha," but awareness and practice of our own gifts will help us gain as much mastery as we can. Often that's far more than we imagined possible.

Further, I discovered that such mindful discipline helped me come to a connection to energy beyond myself which let me flow. This happens because repeating a form frees me. I can put my body and mind into the repetition, so my spirit is free. The heart sutra says form is emptiness and emptiness is form. Let me try to explain how I understand that.

When I repeat a move in Hsing-i again and again, my conscious mind focuses on the form. At first, I may be focusing on moving my feet just so, or I might be working on how to hold my hands. As I become more aware of how the form works, I may play with it a little, try it this way and that way. Gradually it starts to feel right. This is when I sense a connection to spirit; there's a flow of energy that isn't forced but that moves me with fluidity and without forcing. I'm empty and open to this flow.

Why might someone practice a Beethoven sonata again and again? He'll perhaps start by working out the fingering or using a metronome to steady the rhythm. As he becomes familiar with the piece, he may play it differently each time. The music on the page is the same. What is starting to happen is that he brings a different spirit to it each time. He focuses his conscious mind on what he's doing, but then his unconscious mind opens to what I call the energy of the Universe, and he experiences the intuitive flow that brings a performance to a higher level than just plodding through the notes with technical skill. When he really gets it, he may not even remember what he did.

Energy, tapping into spirit, connecting to the Universe is expressed through a form. Why do the Japanese move through the ritual of the tea ceremony? There are the same moves each time. Impatient Westerners ask, "What's the point?" Answer: the point is the energy one is bringing to it at the time. More precisely, I'd say that the energy one brings is actually the energy of the Universe which one is letting flow through oneself and expressing in the form. Moreover, repeating and practicing the form, be it a tea ceremony or Beethoven sonata, is the way one gets to the point that the energy of the Universe can flow through and make the expression beautiful.

So, it's reciprocal. The practice of the form with awareness helps one get in touch with the energy or spirit, and the spirit or energy helps one express the form with mastery.

Let's look at some possible questions. For example, some may say that when our pianist gives an impressive performance, it's just that the spirit moves him, that he may improvise or spontaneously give a dazzling performance, and that jazz musicians improvise all the time.

This may be true, but I don't think someone gets to this point unless he has done plenty of practice first. Even musicians who don't read music listen to other skillful players and study their ways. Certainly, there needs to be room for spontaneity, but, again, to be a master, one needs a basis of practice.

In my case, I found that such mastery lets me be open to how it's best to move (or not move) in any given situation. If I see someone in danger, I don't just slash away and destroy the being smothering him. I can trust that I have the moves and wait for the spirit to make the right move through me. That sounds weird, but sometimes it happens so fast, I don't even know what I'm about to do. That's the difference between mastery and just having the moves.

Is what I'm describing like "being in the zone"? There have been several books written about the athlete who gets into the zone and just takes off without conscious thought. Well, yes, it's like that, but I'm trying to cultivate being in the zone all the time, making the zone larger so there's a spiritual dimension to it. Suppose you're a baseball pitcher and in one game you're in the zone, it's cooking, beautiful, no one can hit you. What did you do to get there? What technique or discipline did you use? Can you do it again? Can you expand it to use it beyond pitching? Can you get to that state chopping wood or drawing water? You can use this approach with Doing (pitching, piano, etc.) or Being (meditating, praying, etc.). My shamanic work is a sense of tantric; that is, I believe anything can be used to get us to a strong connection.

Can this sort of discipline be taught? I've found that you can learn from almost everything. Any book or article or conversation has possibilities if you're alert. It doesn't have to be obvious, like reading about masters or studying with a respected practitioner.

A casual conversation may offer a spark. For example, one person said that he'd thought he was disciplined, and he certainly is, working hard at a demanding job for many years. But when he heard me mention my repeating a move for a year, he realized that his discipline had been outward, making himself do what was necessary to get the job done. It hadn't been inner in the sense of truly developing his abilities.

People may come to me with a psychic gift, but if they're untrained, their energy is scattered, hit or miss. I give different exercises to different people, depending on what they need. I may suggest that one person repeat a mantra, whereas another person may need to pick up her violin and play even if doing so frightens her.

Here's another question: Is my approach to discipline the only way? I've learned that it isn't.

The other day I was talking with Faith (a very gifted healer) and explaining my ideas about discipline, practice, and awareness. She didn't want to contradict me, but she also looked distressed.

I'd been talking about discipline as a daily practice, as a code, as something that warriors do that separates them from fighters. Warriors, I said, have a disciplined practice because it's part of their spiritual way. Fighters may practice the moves and become quite accomplished, but they lack spiritual discipline, the adherence to a code that forms their behavior and even their thoughts. This must have sounded very fierce because Faith finally spoke up.

She used to be shy and unsure, but now, while gentle and considerate, she's learned to believe in her right to speak and in her own power, which is that of a person who can heal others through love.

She took a deep breath and said, "I have a different way. I do my practice when I feel something inside saying, 'let's do this.' Then I want to do it, whatever it is. When I receive that message,

...tice. Then there's no pressure as I would feel with ...of discipline. What I feel is that if I don't do what I feel ...d to do, I won't be successful or complete, won't do what I want to do and what is right for me."

This rocked me, because the thought of waiting until I want to do something just doesn't exist for me. Even as a kid, I loved to practice. I may be sick, but I'll still crawl out of bed to the cushions to meditate. Obviously, however, this way would make Faith feel constrained and lock up the flow of energy for her.

It is hard for me to understand, but this was exciting. I've looked at Faith in action, and at other people who are quite different from me: one, a deeply spiritual and calming presence, and another, an acupuncturist who helps her patients by bringing deep insight to her work with them. I've known that something was happening to them, but I couldn't figure out what enabled them to be so successful when they didn't have the kind of discipline I looked for in masters.

Now it occurred to me that both approaches, Faith's and mine, are similar in that they have a goal.

Faith put it this way: "I came to feel how my energy system works: I feel, I receive, and I Be. So, I wait in my Being until something comes to me and then I act on it. Just to repeat something every day would be a struggle and would induce fear in me."

Unlike Faith's, my energy system is pro-active. I see something and I go at it. It's not that I concentrate on every sword strike or attack every danger. That would be exhausting. But if I take my conscious mind and focus on something, that frees my unconscious mind to expand and let go of thought. I practice a form so that at a certain point, I am Doing; that frees me to connect to Being, to let energy come in and move through me. It's as if I'm not there. I don't think, and if you asked me what I have just done, I wouldn't be able to tell you. I've seen the same process in someone whose gift is working with words. She'll focus on the words, the puzzle, the idea; then she'll go still and pull in the information from somewhere else. She too uses focus, does something, to connect to creativity.

Faith noted that her way of letting Being come in opens her channels of creativity, in her case, dance, painting, and healing. Coming from the opposite way, I end up in a similar creative place. I will focus first. When I sit on the cushions and focus every day, the experience is always different. This too is creativity. I create new things all the time. Sometimes I get up and move, sometimes I get a flash of what's going on with a client, sometimes I'm just doing Ho'o Pono Pono, saying, "I love you."

What seems to happen with Faith and people like her is that first they connect to Being and then they get to Doing. They don't start with focus. They start with letting themselves just Be, getting to a quiet place of receptivity. Their practice is to be open to Being. I've seen how hard Faith has worked to learn to get to this quiet state.

There's discipline here too. And when these people come to a quiet place of receptivity, when they then sense what is needed, then they Do. When they hear what to do, they do it, and with noteworthy discipline.

So, Faith and I are actually on the same spectrum; we're just on opposite extreme ends of it. Amazing.

When I announce with such conviction that we need discipline, people ask, "Why?"

My answer is, "The reason is that we need to practice. And the reason to practice is to connect with the Universe. And with such connection we find the balance we need at any given time."

Even with such discipline, however, there was still something that kept me from fully coming to terms with the violence within. I still feared it. Therefore, I resisted looking at it as deeply as I needed to.

Resistance I

Before I go on with my personal story, and this seeming digression may be more of my resistance, I'd like to look in a more general way at how resistance works and how it hinders us.

I first got the idea of resistance from what I observed in my shamanic healing practice. It is a big part of what I see keeping people back. I try to sense what a patient is resisting, what's blocking his ability to let go and simply (well, maybe not so simply) connect with the energy of the Universe. It may be that the person is resisting what he really needs. For example, hesitating to leave a house when a person needs to move may make him sick. In this case, fear is causing resistance. Another kind of resistance is at play when someone holds back from following his gift, perhaps because a soul is taking his energy for herself or because a parent's voice may be saying that he is incompetent or because he fears failure or fears success. A desire to manipulate may keep a woman from having an open loving relationship. My job is to help people release their resistance.

The phrase "energy of the Universe" may not be your way of thinking. I don't care whether your conceptual framework is the energy studied by physicists, God, or a neurochemical network. It's all the same. It doesn't matter how you think of it.

Using my image, think of the Universe's energy as an electric current. Electricity flows best when there is least resistance; fiber optic cables can carry more than the older copper wires because there's less resistance. Similarly, we function best when energy flows through us without the resistance caused by fear, anger, dislike of self, excessive excitement, or possession. Another analogy might be the religious concept of doing the will of God; devout people work and pray hard to open themselves to the will of God and not to let their own desires or fears control their actions.

In this chapter, first I'd like to examine perhaps the most common form of resistance: resisting the darker parts of oneself. Then I want to discuss another kind of resistance, one that comes with and intensifies imbalance.

That first, most common kind of resistance is not acknowledging the darker parts of oneself. We don't like to think of ourselves as angry, passive, or selfish. This is hardly a new idea. Jung, for example, wrote brilliantly about the shadow self, and about the power of owning the darker parts of oneself. Let me give you a classic case from my practice in the patient's own version.

"It all began with my trying to deal with anger. I sent John an email: 'When I'm confronted by an angry person, I feel my stomach knot. I almost teared up when a policeman pulled me over and berated me for going ten miles an hour over the speed limit. I wanted to hit a neighbor when she berated me for something my wife had done. When I was trying to mediate a dispute in a role play (not even in real life!) and one of the parties attacked me for not protecting her, I froze and had to be rescued by the trainer.'

"I was looking for instant analysis and cure, but John's reply was in general terms. He wrote back to me, 'The only thing I have come up with is to find the part of you that is reacting that way.

Talk with that part, ask him what's going on, spend time loving him until the emotion is gone. Interesting.'

"'Interesting' was an understatement, so I tried psychological analysis and wrote John again. 'I think the fear of anger comes from the intensity of my father's anger when he came at me and my siblings. But knowing this hasn't helped.'"

"John replied tersely, 'It's not your father who is the problem now. There's part of you that needs to be healed.'

"Uh oh. It was easier to analyze my father, but I'll try it John's way. I meditated, saw visions of a black shaft going through my heart, and tried to interpret the image, but nothing explained my problems with anger. Maybe something was happening at a deeper level, though, because one day I had a total meltdown into sadness. A kind friend listened as I admitted one of my deepest fears. I'd always tried to be brave and had coped with whatever was happening to me, including death of a wife and loss of a job. But now without external structure, I fear there was nothing inside me, just hollow, fundamental inadequacy.

"I wanted John to reassure me, but again he tossed it back to me. 'Remember that the idea is to love whatever part of yourself you are seeing or feeling. Before you see, call in the connection to love and try to keep that with you as you go.'

"'Yeah, sure,' I thought. 'Love myself, which I'm discovering is totally unlovable, which is just a phony hollow shell.'

"At our next small group meeting, I burst out with, 'How can I love parts of me that I hate? I hate my fearfulness! I hate my own anger!'

"The next blow was my friend, who'd been kind about listening when I had the meltdown. He told me he didn't want to get together anymore. I didn't know why and was very hurt.

"I asked John, 'What did I do wrong or hadn't seen?'" His answer took me to yet a more painful level. No comfort or softening of the blow there. The first line of his email was, 'You have a lot of your father in you.' I was devastated. John was saying I was like this man who had caused me such pain, whom I'd tried so hard not to be like.

"John went on, 'When you get into trouble, you become more like him. Rageful, cold, hard, unforgiving. You know what he is like. You become him. This is not you at all, but this is what I see. I think this is what happened with your friend. You became your father. Though you weren't raging at your friend but at other stuff in your life. He couldn't take the intensity of your anger. It reminded him of his mother. In a way it was good he could recognize the problem and protect himself. But too bad he couldn't confront it and separate you from your father.'

"Continuing, John said, 'I've been working to keep your father away from you, but please work on loving the part of you that becomes your father. The love is what he hates, and it will heal you.'

"Though grateful for John's time and work, I was horrified. I'd always thought of myself as basically kind, and here he was saying I was like my father in exactly those ways I hated in him. And they were inside me. I felt unclean, as if there were infected, corrupt spots in me that I couldn't get out. As I sat at my computer reading what John had written, I felt self-pity, confusion, and the fragile hope that we could work on it. I was confused and fragile."

"John made another attempt to sort things out. 'You are not him. You are not him. You let that part of you that is your father take over. By loving yourself, you undo all that and become you.'

"Huh? If there's part of me that is like him, then that is me. Right then I hated him.

"Another instruction from John, 'Send your rage back to him before you do the Ho'o Pono Pono. You can visualize it or write it, but you must send it back to him. We have to get it off you. You will not harm him. It's the rage that is holding the two of you together.'

"So, I wrote and wrote, pounding the keys, yelling at my father for the screaming fights when he'd come at us children with black rage. Yelling at him for manipulating me into serving him and for getting inside me and corrupting me. I can't quote here what I wrote because I went out into the backyard and burned the pages.

"The catharsis certainly felt good and helped, but there was no magic cure. The work was long and hard. I had periods of rage when my father conned me into giving up time to help him and times when I just wanted to fade into 'easeful death.' The kicker was that as I separated from him, I felt the loss of what was familiar even though it had been harmful. Even though I hadn't wanted my father near me, when I started to loosen the connection and John kept working to move him away, I missed what I was used to and didn't know how to be or act.

"I finally got to the point of realizing that it was my fault that people shied away from me. I wrote, 'It's all up to me, always has been, always is, eh. I just didn't want it to be.'

"John answered, 'That's the essence of the whole thing. For all of us.' Then he added, 'No fault. No fault. Just what is. Love the fault, the rage, the whole thing. It is actually freeing. If it is all up to you, then you can change the whole thing. Hard but freeing.'

"The work continues, but I feel as if I'm seeing more clearly, and the heavy blackness in my heart has been wrapped in white gauze."

As his resistance to acknowledging the anger in himself and as the attachment to his father has faded, Robert's rage has lessened and his ability to love has become stronger.

One thing that puzzled Robert was the idea of loving the parts of himself that he hated. How can that be? It's not love in the sense of admiration or desire or wanting something. It's more like the love of compassion. Furthermore, when we feel compassionate towards someone or something, first we acknowledge *it is the way it is*. If we see clearly, we can accept without judging.

Easy to say, but how do we come to see clearly and to accept? Understand that not loving oneself, not having compassion for our difficult parts, may be a resistance that comes from our past. When Robert felt threatened, all he could hear was his father screaming and coming at him with great ferocity. Okay, that anger was in his father. What stayed in Robert was the memory of that experience.

As a result, when Robert felt threatened, he felt fear and then he reacted like his father with coldness or rage. What is at the deeper level in Robert, what is really his, is fear. That's what's his. What's underneath the fear? Something that comes from his childhood mind, an old memory of being terrified when his father came at him.

What to do? If he comes to understand and accept this dynamic, the next time Robert is in a situation that evokes this feeling, he may not just withdraw coldly or get angry; he may be more directly aware of the fear and not automatically respond to it with his father's kind of anger. If he can see and accept the rage without judging, he'll be able to see and accept the fear without judging.

The metaphor I keep coming back to is that this is like cleaning a mirror from the emotional baggage from the past. Another image is that the original experience is like a dot. When one becomes aware of the layers—in this case, rage covering fear—the dot itself loses power and disappears.

Here's another example of someone resisting what seems to be her less lovely side. I had a patient who was a psychic healer. In addition to her skill in this area, she was usually very analytical and clear thinking. Once a month, however, before and during her menstrual period, she would suffer with depression, cramps, bad headaches, any kind of darkness you can think of. She hated that because then she couldn't be the kind of logical thinker she wanted to be.

I thought there had to be a reason along with, maybe behind, the physical explanations because I was picking up more than just physical causes.

"Maybe it's a place of power for you," I suggested.

"Are you nuts?" she responded. "Look at me, I'm a mess."

Still, since she was suffering so much and hadn't found relief in the usual medical approaches, she agreed to try another approach.

For her, the issue was to accept that her body, mind, and emotions change every month and not only to be okay with that but actually to find power in it. Instead of suggesting that she try to love the darkness with the intention to get rid of it, I suggested that she embrace it, go into it, ask it, "Who are you? What are you here for? How can I be with you?"

At first tentatively, then with more confidence, when she went into what she felt as the darkness during her period, she tried not to resist or lament or fear it. As a result, during that time she became someone whose dominant mode was feeling, someone whose perceptions came through inarticulate sensing, not through her usual logical thinking. She doesn't get headaches and cramps anymore, just gets a little spacey because she's having amazing insights. Then when her period is over, she can use the other, logical, part of her to implement these insights.

For example, in spite of her professional skills, she hadn't been able to figure out how to get patients. When she let herself go into the dark place, let herself feel what she was feeling, she got ideas of how to reach out to people. Later, when her period was over, she could make phone calls, contact people, and set up appointments. Before this, she was frozen, and even if you gave her a list of what to do to attract patients, she couldn't do it. Now she could intuitively receive information that she'd blocked when she was in the bright analytical place. Now she could use the power of both sides of herself. She has achieved some balance between the dark or intuitive and the light or analytical sides of herself. Not simultaneously but skillfully using each.

These are two examples of people resisting what they see as weaknesses or undesirable parts of themselves. In contrast to those who turn away from their difficulties, another kind of resistance comes when people get out of balance by going too far into their strengths.

Let me start by referring to a couple of situations mentioned earlier in the two chapters on fear. When Vesta was attacked by her father, she was so loving, so in her heart that the arrow he shot at her stuck in her. She froze for two reasons: first, because of memories and emotional history. They were part of her resistance. If she didn't have that remembered pain and fear, his barb might have gone through her without harm. She could have thought, "He's just an old man, afraid he's going to die, acting crazy, so he's lashing out in an old pattern." The other reason Vesta froze was that she was stuck in her own pattern of trying to meet everything with love; she was out of balance. She resists giving up her pattern of love. What she needs to do is to balance love with focus. To protect herself, she needs to focus, to notice when the loving energy is so huge that she doesn't see a threat coming; she needs to stop and look, not just try to love whoever or whatever is coming at her.

Ariel has yet another pattern of resistance. Because her greatest gift is hyperfocusing, she looks for patterns and analyzes them. Also, she overcompensates her strength: she can get stuck in a pattern, she can see too much; her brain goes round and round until she gets lost. Her focus becomes so intense that she is resisting the flow that calm can allow. Then she can't just ride the energy and let it guide her to understanding; she obsesses, gets caught in details and possibilities.

An additional complication is she has a big heart. As was the case with Vesta, when Ariel's siblings came at her, she got stuck in her fear and froze. She opened her heart, hoping that there could just be simple love between her and her brother and sister. What she needs to do is be aware (remember the importance of awareness?) when her heart comes in and she's feeling loving; and then monitor that with the seeing. Then she can both focus and be loving, thus gaining the balance she needs between the two.

I've talked about connecting with the energy of the Universe. It is a good thing. Paradoxically, it can also knock one off balance. Take the case of Donavan. A group of us had a drumming workshop, with a great musician using many kinds of drums and gongs, a wild range of rhythms and pitches, to raise the levels of energy. Many people started moving spontaneously. Religious dancers, dervishes, do the same thing to connect. At our drumming session, Donavan danced ecstatically for three hours. I could see him on a cliff by the Irish sea, long hair blowing in the fierce wind, calling in the spirits. He loved the energy, the intensity, the excitement.

Donavan can use this energy in his role as a healer, but when he connects, he often loses control. The energy gets overwhelming for him. He gets so overwhelmed that he can't function; he feels the pain of others and then the pain of the world and sobs and sobs. When he feels joy, it gets to be too much, and he cries and cries. He can't find a mate because he scares potential partners. Either he overwhelms them with love, or he gets so caught in his idea that this is the perfect woman, he can't talk. He has no problem attracting women because he's handsome and personable, but when he's drawn to a woman, there's a huge rush of energy coming out at her, and she pulls away.

To calm such intensity, he uses marijuana and alcohol and food. He's starting to realize that being out on the extremes of energy isn't working for him. He's in his late thirties and recovering takes him longer than it used to. Moreover, when he crashes, he can't connect to energy at all and then can't do his healing work because he's so exhausted.

I try to tell him that in a place of balance, there's a different kind of excitement. Instead of ratcheting the energy up to an extreme—ecstatic seeing or overwhelming feeling, immobilized Being or out of control Doing—you can let the energy of the Universe flow through you. True, the extremes are exciting and even addictive. But at one's place of balance, Being and Doing mix together, flowing through you. It's very intense but also very calm. It's peaceful but not static. The energy moves and changes and flows. It's a clear and peaceful space.

Maybe it's partly that as you get older, you can't handle the extremes as well—either the huge vibration of Doing or the huge absorption of Being. After all, as a young man Buddha lived in a palace where he could overwhelm himself with pleasures; then he went to the extreme of asceticism. And maybe you have to go through the excitements a few—or many—times to realize that they don't get you to that deep connection to the Universe.

People who come to me are there because they want that total connection. Donavan connects on the extremes with no problem, but he knows that he's still not happy. That intensity is not good enough for him; he wants something more. People may have different goals. For some in this lifetime, the goal may be to be Kierkegaard's aesthetic man, loving the perfect meal or the most exquisite concert. Or it may be to live according to the highest standards of society, as an ethical person. Or it may be to reach deep intellectual understanding. For me, intellectual discussions are nice, but I need the experiential kind of thing too. When I look for an answer, I don't think it; I go into my experience and see it and feel it and act on it.

What's my current understanding of the balanced place, and how have I come to that? It's not been easy. My own fears and resistances have been formidable.

Resistance II

The time came for me to face up to my own resistance. What kept me from letting the energy of the Universe flow through me easily? The simple answer: violence.

So many of my memories and interactions have been about violence. This crazy energy has always been there, in my past lives and now. When I talk about crazy energy, I don't mean just the dark power that I have and can use to attack dangers and that I call on to help people who are being threatened or harmed. When I call this dark energy "crazy," I mean that it gets out of control, starts to vibrate so strongly that either I must let it out physically or I turn it inward so as not to hurt others, and then I get sick.

In one past life, for example, I was a Spanish knight who murdered people who crossed me or were in my way. When I was in this state of needing to release the crazy energy, I was not only likely to go out and attack, I was also easily manipulated by certain people to carry out what they wanted done. A past-life lover would tell me that someone was threatening her, so I'd go attack him. After all, when you're out of control, you're in the grip of strong emotion and thus not aware and balanced; you're not thinking clearly or alert to what others may be doing to you surreptitiously. In my current life, when I was younger, the energy would build in me and I'd start vibrating and would just have to release it, so I'd pick someone up and throw him. A man who was in my Gung Fu club at Harvard recently told me that he remembered my saying to other guys, "I'm going to punch and you're going to try to stop me." They couldn't, as I'd known they couldn't, and I'd plaster them against the wall.

Because of this history both in past lives and in this life, I've been afraid of my dark power to attack. I've feared either that I'd hurt others or that others would take advantage of me and use my energy for their own purposes. My shamanic teacher kept saying to me, "No violence." This was a useful lesson because it made me more aware of the dangerous tendency for my energy to get crazy. It was an early step in observing when the energy got crazy and then trying to learn why and how this happens.

When I started thinking deeply about where this energy comes from and what it is, I first thought there was violent energy that I attracted, an energy that comes to me. But then I thought, I'm not always crazy. There are plenty of times that I'm loving or calm or in control. It's not as if I'm attracting just violent energy. There are times when I attach to the energy of the Universe and I'm fine. So, it's not that the energy that comes to me is always violent or crazy.

Moreover, people who are Love Healers also use the energy of the Universe, and through them it may have great power, power which certainly is not violent. So, it followed that either different energy comes to me at various times, or there are as many different kinds of energy as there are people or types of people—or something else is going on.

I concluded, "No, it doesn't make sense that there are millions of distinct kinds of energy. All energy is just energy, not tinged in this way or that way." As I explained in *Voices from the Other Side of the Couch*, the energy of the Universe is just that, neutral energy. It may come through an individual differently at various times. It comes out differently in different people. The energy moves through some people as love, through others as intellectual power, through yet others as violence.

The next question had to be, "Okay what was going on when I lost control or got violent?" Digging deeper, I realized that this crazy energy builds most easily when I get excited or angry. When that happens, either I express it in a very physical yang way, or when I don't express the energy outwardly, I get sick. At a gathering a few years ago, I was excited to see people I'd not seen for many years. Because I got so excited, my energy was all over the place, not focused and used in a controlled way. Moreover, I wasn't watching, wasn't seeing, and so didn't protect myself. As a result, I didn't see people coming at me with old stories of the way I used to be. The stories and the emotional intensity of being with long lost friends affected me without my realizing it. It was no coincidence that shortly after this event, I got sick with a long-lasting flu.

The sequence seemed to be that the energy comes in, I get excited, thus building resistance. Remember that by resistance I mean anything that keeps the energy of the Universe from flowing easily and freely through me. The excitement seems to do this to me. When that happens, I don't see what's going on within me or outside of me; so, the energy builds and I get out of balance.

I connected this perception with what I knew from my long practice with T'ai Chi. In T'ai Chi, when you are tense or tight, you resist the energy that is coming at you from your sparring partner or opponent. When this happens, the opponent can knock you down. When you don't resist, nothing happens, you just sense the flow of energy and move with it. I discovered that sometimes I blocked the flow while doing T'ai Chi: when I was sparring, and I was starting to get out of control, all I wanted to do was stick a spear in someone. My partners recognized when the energy started to build because I got this wild look in my eyes and grin on my face.

I found that when I got to that point, I could stop, become aware, and do what would eliminate the resistance. For me that meant using love to bring me back to balance. When I start getting crazy, I start doing Ho'o Pono Pono. I say to myself, "I love you." Doing so eliminates the resistance.

To use my favorite metaphor again, the excess of ferocity or anger or fear is like dust gathering on a mirror. Stopping and saying "I love you" clears the emotion like cleaning the dust off a mirror. The sparring becomes effortless, there's a gentle flow of energy, and then no one can touch me.

Since I've gotten more aware of the dynamic, and since I've been working on coming from the heart, balancing force with love, I now have less reaction to things that used to set me off and make me crazy. Instead, there is more often balance, which lets the energy of the Universe flow through without resistance.

Furthermore, this thinking about resistance has led me to understand that what I do is perceive resistance. That's when I'm most successful at sparring. I sense the resistance in an opponent and without even thinking just move toward it.

When I reached this stage of understanding, a curious thing happened, confirming that by striving for balance and lessening resistance, I was gaining more power. Dark Aphrodites started appearing. To explain what I mean, I need to lay out the dynamic that exists between me and Aphrodites.

Aphrodites

As I was becoming more powerful, the kind of women I call Aphrodites were appearing more frequently in my practice and my life. Women like this are attracted to men they want to manipulate into doing their wishes. Obviously, the more powerful the man, the more likely he is to succeed in whatever task the Aphrodite wants accomplished.

I had to be careful when these Aphrodites started popping up because I've been susceptible to Aphrodites in past lives and in my early manhood in this life. One reason is that like everyone else, I have emotional, psychological, and psychic weaknesses. For me, a big concern is being sucked in to help and protect Aphrodites in a way that is not good for them or for me. I just want to dash in and do what they lure me to do.

One result of the weakness in our makeup, for all of us, is that we're susceptible to certain people's energy that plays on our weakness. We tend to fall into the same traps over and over, keep getting slammed over and over until we deal with the issue. Why? Because we resist seeing our weakness, we don't want to admit them, or we are so used to the pattern that we don't recognize the way it's destructive for us.

Here's an example that I see repeatedly in my practice. A patient had no connection with her mother because the mother had given her no nurturing and had turned away when she needed anything. My patient was in a position of authority over a group in her office, including the responsibility of evaluating her subordinates. One person in this group was like the patient's mother. Whenever my patient met this woman, the woman avoided her, and my patient would lose her composure. The connection to her past with her mother seems obvious, right? But in fact, she resists seeing that this is what's going on, resists seeing her susceptibility to this kind of woman, and even if she sees it, she doesn't know how to change the connection.

Okay, my weakness is Aphrodites. Who are these women? Aphrodites are women who have an energy that draws men in. Think of the movie divas who can manipulate men to do what they want, like the woman in an old film who got a man to murder her husband for her. Saul Bellow said of Marilyn Monroe, "She was connected with a powerful current, but she couldn't disconnect herself from it....She had a kind of curious incandescence under the skin" (quoted by Maureen Dowd, *New York Times*, Oct. 19, 2010).

Here's a more everyday example: one sunny day I was sitting on the front steps of my office building with a patient who has this power. Across the street, in front of the library, were a couple of men talking with each other. I said to her,

"See those guys across the street? Make the one in the red shirt come over."

She just looked at them with a little smile, then turned back to talking with me. Five minutes later the guy in the red shirt came over with a question about directions.

It's not a matter of being beautiful or dressing provocatively. The power of Aphrodites is internal. There is a physical lure that they have, call it biology, chemicals, pheromones, or what you will. That's just the way they are, just as from birth I was a warrior or as someone else is gifted with the power of healing. We've all seen little girls who simply know how to flirt. We don't blame them for it. What grown Aphrodites are accountable for, like everyone else, is the way they use their power.

Aphrodites can use their power creatively, for example, to be artists and actors, to light up a room, to lead their children lovingly. Since I'm susceptible to the enticements of Aphrodites in ways that aren't so good for me or for them, what I describe below emphasizes ways that they can use their power to lure people, the kind of lure that in the past has made me want to rush in and do as they wish.

In addition to the physical lure, Aphrodites also pull people in by manipulating their needs. How do they do this? Most people have a need to serve others in one way or another. Some need to love; some need to heal; some need to nurture; some, like me, need to protect. Others need to do something else. Whatever this desire to serve is, Aphrodites can manipulate it, so that when you do what they want, you feel totally validated and needed. If you need to protect, for example, an Aphrodite can get you to feel that if you disconnect from someone she wants out of the way, you are being her great protector. A skillful Aphrodite will find someone whose needs will serve her particular needs.

Not all Aphrodites use this power destructively. There are degrees. Those I call light Aphrodites are interested in manipulation and drama. You do what they want because you want their love. An example might be the good witch in *The Wizard of Oz*. I heard about a woman who cared very much about teaching her children to eat in a healthful way. There are many ways for mothers to do this, such as having only healthy food in the house, teaching kids in an age-appropriate way how to make good choices, planting a garden, setting an example, or pointing out dangers of too much sugar and fat. This Aphrodite told her kids, "I love you, and if you love me, you won't eat sugar." There wasn't overt sexuality here, she felt genuine maternal love for her kids, but there was some sort of covert pull. There would be a hug and a kiss, telling the children, "What a good boy you are, what a good girl you are." She used their desire to please her. There's some sort of emotional tug. It will work with boys and with non-Aphrodite girls. (Aphrodite girls tend to clash with their mothers.) When I point out the dynamic to a light Aphrodite, she will get it and can learn to notice when she's using her power manipulatively in ways that are not good for her or others. I can kid with her.

Of course, there are also dark Aphrodites, like the wicked witch in *The Wizard of Oz*. At worst, these dark Aphrodites want to suck your energy, to manipulate, to feed on your energy. At best, they want someone who's powerful, calm, confident, someone who can give them a sense of protection. But they go about getting this sense of safety by manipulating and draining the man's energy. They believe they need warriors. But think about the wisdom in some of our culture's deepest roots.

Aphrodite, the beautiful, alluring Greek goddess of love, was married to Hephaestus, the ugly, crippled smith of the gods. He adored her and was a steady and invaluable worker, but who did she want? She wanted—and got—Ares, the god of war. We know what kinds of trouble can happen when love attaches to warlike strength and aggression. Guinevere was married to Arthur, the legendary British king who tried to bring peace and justice to his feuding kingdom, the leader who developed a code of the strong helping the weak. Whom did Guinevere want and have an affair with? Lancelot, the greatest warrior among Arthur's knights. Their affair contributed to rifts, lack of trust, and the undermining of ideals that ultimately led to the downfall of Arthur's kingdom. We recognize the pattern; there's a reason the story of Camelot, Arthur's kingdom, endures even today in plays, a musical, political allusions. (Though the presidential Kennedy Camelot was not toppled by infidelity on the part of Jackie, or Jack's extensive philandering for that matter, there was the sense of the fragility of such a dazzling time with bigger than life-size figures. And Jackie did later marry one of the richest and most powerful men in the world, among other reasons, reportedly to gain protection for her children.)

Going back even further into our western history, consider the story of Gilgamesh and Innana, the goddess of love in the Sumerian/Babylonian cultures. After Gilgamesh, the part-divine king of Sumer, had triumphed over the demon of the forest, Innana propositioned him. Unlike Ares and Lancelot, Gilgamesh understood the situation. He wisely turned her down, because she was notorious for using and then discarding her lovers. She reacted by inflicting huge floods on the people and by killing Gilgamesh's dearest friend and fellow warrior, Enkidu.

The best mate for Aphrodites is actually a steady, loving person. When they go after a powerful man, whether they get him or not, they can cause huge problems.

As I said, Aphrodites have been popping up recently in my life. Here's an example of one. Last week I saw a woman who'd consulted me four or five years ago. She's a powerful seer, divorced, with two daughters. She came back to me because she said she saw dark, powerful things taking over her house, threatening her daughters. She wanted me to clear her house, protect her kids, and bring her some sense of safety. But her way of getting what she wanted would have eventually sucked the life out of me. Dark Aphrodites like me because they believe they can't break me.

They think they can keep taking and taking. This woman would call me whenever she got afraid; she'd ask me to come in and clear the house. I knew that if I kept responding and doing what she wanted, I'd get exhausted. What I had to help her see was that she was the one attracting dark forces and that therefore she was going to have to change. I couldn't just rush in and save her. To her credit, she realized that since she'd been to ten shamans and none of them had carried out what she wanted, the problem was with her. That's brilliant and courageous.

Men tend to fear Aphrodites because their power makes men feel manipulated, tempted, and weak. It makes sense that the myths and lore, which dramatize the dangers of powerful women, were written by men, and mostly by men in patriarchal, warrior cultures. Well, I'm a warrior, and in the past, I've fallen into the trap.

There's a powerful Aphrodite, the only person I know who can be lying flat on her back, in pain, not leaving her house, and still wanting someone to marry her. In our past lives, there was a huge erotic attraction between us; I was the one with the warrior power, and she would manipulate me to use it in ways that she wanted. After being out of touch for four years, she suddenly called me. Canny, she tested the waters by asking whether I'd help someone else she knew, but I could see that though this might have been true, she was also trying to pull me back into helping her in many ways. So, I said, "Better not."

Other Aphrodites in my practice have started acting up, wanting me to serve their needs directly rather than help them learn to find better ways to care for themselves. An Aphrodite in another state has been emailing that she wants me to be big and strong and to come rescue her from her fears and angers. She tells me that when I get into all this Ho'o Pono Pono stuff, love and light, I'm just being a wimp.

On the contrary, as I said earlier, before this discussion of Aphrodites, since I've worked to learn loving energy, I've gained more balance and thus have become stronger. The Aphrodites started coming back into my life precisely because I was becoming more powerful.

What I've been learning is that I need to be aware of what's going on and not respond to the enticements, both to protect myself and to enable me to stay steady so I can help the Aphrodites who come to me. If they can manipulate me, it might please them, but it won't really do them any good; they'll just keep wanting more and more from someone outside themselves. If I can see what's going on and send love to the part of me that's tempted, lo and behold, I don't get manipulated. I need to maintain my own balance whatever comes at me, whether temptation or attack. Despite realizing this, however, I still had a way to go before getting a fuller picture of what balance meant.

Resistance III

For all the progress I was making, I was still afraid that people would take advantage of me, as the Aphrodites were circling and trying to do. I also still had trouble accepting the tendency toward violence. Though I often used dark power constructively to attack what might be harming someone, such as a soul that was sucking someone's health, I knew it could hurt people too if I felt under threat. I feared that it could blaze out and harm, not be under my rational control. Furthermore, I knew that there was a danger of getting addicted to my power, for I loved the way I felt when I just moved fast and conquered.

In spite of all such awareness, there was the old problem: I couldn't just restrain the impulse to violence and instinct to attack. When I tried to hold all that energy in and be loving, it wasn't healthy for me, and I'd just get sick.

So, the next step was to try to be balanced, to feel both the warrior energy and the loving energy. What I tried to do was bring up loving energy to be as strong as the warrior energy (see the chapter on Ho'o Pono Pono). When I got the two in balance, there was calm, peace. When I got to this calm place, the energy of the Universe seemed to follow my intent. I'd look at a situation, see what needed to be done, and then the energy would flow through me. At this point, the image I had was of dark aggressive energy at one extreme and light loving energy at the other. I tried to be in the middle. When it worked, I felt as if I were in the middle, balanced; and a column seemed to go up, as if there were pure spirit ascending.

To my distress, however, this approach didn't always work as well as I hoped it would. Try as I might to move to a place of love, I still got sick or hurt. I thought that I just needed to work harder for a balance of love and ferocity (the dark energy I use when I need to attack something harmful). Further, I figured that since I wasn't in balance all the time, I needed to express this dark side of me in the everyday world, say through sparring, learning to shoot a rifle, or practicing with a sword. I hoped that such strong, aggressive action might keep the dark energy from building up so much that it would start vibrating and causing trouble. I thought I had the matter figured out: release the aggressive energy through sparring, etc., call on loving energy, and reach a balance between the warrior energy and the loving energy. Problem solved. I just needed to work harder.

Wrong.

Severe muscle spasms let me know that something was still amiss. I was hit with excruciating pain in my hip. I couldn't get up out of a chair without agony; I couldn't walk without needing to sit down every few feet. Yes, this was physical pain with a physical cause. I saw doctors, had tests, and did all the usual things to address such pain, but I knew that wasn't enough. I was sure that there was something underlying the physical problem, something I needed to understand and deal with.

One day when I was meeting with a couple of people in my office, I was sitting in my big black chair as usual but wincing whenever I moved. Hope was sitting on the comfortable green couch across from me. As usual, she was looking warm and lovely with her blue eyes, soft gray bangs, woven shawl, and turquoise jewelry.

More quickly and directly than was her wont, she leaned forward and said, "Maybe it's not a matter of getting a balance that's in the middle. You've been trying for an equal balance of violence and love. Your image was of love at one end of a spectrum and violence at the other; you visualized balance as being in the middle. You thought this was the way you get to that feeling of connection to the Universe, when the energy flows through you without resistance. And maybe this does happen sometimes.

"I see it differently. Look, John. Your core is that you're a warrior, and you're not okay with that. You fight it, you try to be as loving as you are aggressive. But you are who you are. The warrior in you attacked your hip and caused the muscle spasms."

The light dawned. She was right. I was still afraid of the ferocity in me, the warrior who would attack whatever was coming at me or at someone I was caring for. I realized that I had to accept and love the fact that my core energy is violent and dark. In fact, I'd been attacking the very part of me that is strongest.

Aha, I thought. Balance doesn't just mean being in the middle. Rather, picture a continuum from ferocity to loving. Maybe instead of thinking the middle is the place to be, I need to think of there being a sort of meter which may move to one side or another. Balance isn't just being in the middle. It's being where you need to be on that spectrum at a given time. I realized I had to let go of the fear of my own nature.

Now, the question was, "Can I hold that dark nature in me, embrace it, without hating or fearing it?"

What would help was that I also have the code of the warrior, and part of that code is to use my energy and skills responsibly.

Honoring this code helps keep me and others safe. I don't know why the code is there, but it is. It's also helpful that often when someone walks in and I see someone or something that I feel I need to attack, I can wait and sense whether I'm called to do something. I don't just rush in every time even though it's hard to pause when people want me to deliver fireworks right away.

But if I just let the dark energy go out, maybe there will be times when I can't control it. That's scary; I needed to think about this some more.

The woman who helped me to take the next step in thinking about all this is deeply loving, the embodiment of the mother, the earth nurturer. That's what her core is. Her instinct is to respond to the pain of others by just rushing in and loving them. But, she said, doing so all the time can exhaust her or leave her vulnerable to getting used or hurt; it can also be the wrong move for the person she wants to help. She gave an example from her own experience. When she was working at her store the other day, a man came in and went to the other end of the room. She was busy and so at first just assumed he was browsing. When he was quiet for several minutes, she went over to ask whether she could help. As she rounded the corner, she saw that he was in tears. Her impulse was to go and hug him, but instead she asked, "Would you like a hug?" He said "Yes," so then she hugged him. She didn't turn away from her impulse or wish it wasn't there or repress it out of fear.

She does sometimes fear that her nature will get her hurt or will be manipulated or attacked by others, but she realizes that this is who she is. It won't help her to deny her nature by withdrawing or by trying to be as fierce as she is loving.

She says that she sees her energy as a column of light going up. When she resists it, she sees dark orbs around it, like weights, and she feels dark heavy weight around her. When she can just be in her place of power, which for her is pure love and light, the weight drops away. For me, when I resist being in my power, I get that feeling of vibration building. But that doesn't mean we should try to be other than who we are.

Okay, I thought, what does this mean I need to do? I do need to let the energy out, but it's crucial that I not stay there, that I just let it out and not get addicted. And I need to stop trying to love it away. Ho'o Pono Pono doesn't work for reducing that dark energy or to quiet the warrior in me. What I should use it for is to practice love, so I don't let the energy get tight. If all I do is go with the warrior, the energy will get vibrating. An analogy would be a weightlifter who only lifts. He's going to get tight and muscle-bound. He needs also to work on flexibility. I need to work on loving, including having love and compassion for my basic nature, because love and light are not my natural way. Understatement: I don't need to work on the warrior energy.

So, was this the answer: be who you are, stay in your power? Well, it's a little more complicated than that. It's not as if there's a fixed way to be all the time. We all look for certainty and a fixed pattern or answer. In sparring, I want things all lined up and perfect, but then they'll shift. It's important in sparring, or anything else, for that matter, that I'm always in motion, shifting, scanning, looking for an opening in an opponent's defense, looking around a patient for something that's not quite right. When I've focused on what's going on and seen what's needed, the energy will come out in a perfect straight line and do what it needs to do.

This holds for other kinds of power too. For example, Rebecca loves clear patterns with words, books that have a well-structured argument or plot, an idea that makes clear sense. When she and I sit down to talk about an idea or a problem, she'll ask questions, ask whether this or that is what I mean; she'll come at me from different angles, trying to get clear on what I'm really meaning. Then there may come a moment when she gets it, "Aha, I can see it now," and then she'll articulate the point exactly.

So far, so good, but there was yet another level of understanding. I approached it because I met a hawk. Brother Hawk.

Brother Hawk

This May my wife and I stopped for a couple of days in Manchester, Vermont. The leaves were about halfway out, making the trees lacy, and the weather was still crisp, the sun not too hot; in fact, earlier that week it had snowed a little. One morning, Laura laughed, because she knew how I'd react, and said she'd noticed that there was a school nearby called The British School of Falconry. That was all I needed to know.

We called and made an appointment for the same day. Given how eager I was, we were lucky that it was too early for there to be many tourists.

Falconry is an old hunting sport. The Egyptians as well as the Babylonians hunted with trained birds of prey. It was also popular in the European Middle Ages among the noble class. In fact, it was part of a knight's training to learn how to hunt with a bird. As I was to discover, this training for future warriors involved not only using the bird to hunt but also assimilating the way the bird hunted.

The trainer and I stood at the edge of a large field. She put a big, padded glove on my left hand. The hawk had a tether on its leg to hold while it was resting on my arm. The first part of the training was learning how to cast the hawk into the wind and call it back. Around the field were perches about twenty feet high for the hawk to land on, horizontal bars where it would stay until it was called back.

The first time I called him back, the hawk landed on my arm. It was an amazing high. His approach and landing took my breath away. The bird had a three-foot wingspan and came in at a fast speed. I thought he would knock me over. But the hawk weighed only two and a half pounds and was amazingly agile in the air. Brother Hawk stopped on a dime and landed lightly on my glove.

Beyond this brief high, the most amazing and lasting thing for me was my ability to communicate with Brother Hawk. He and I became one from the beginning.

The first connection I saw was that he scans the landscape, looking for movement. When there's movement, he's drawn to it, his eye focuses on it. If the prey makes the smallest rustle in the grass, he attacks. If the prey can freeze and stay immobile, he doesn't see it. When there's no movement, he scans elsewhere. I'm the same way. I search for darkness and for patterns that are not what they should be. When I see dark forces or disruptions in a smooth pattern, I'm drawn to them. If there's a layer of possession covering someone's own energy pattern, if a person is trembling with fear, if someone's stuck in a dark cave unable to get to the lighted sea beyond, I focus on that. If no disharmony in the pattern exists, I move on.

What struck me most, however, was that Brother Hawk's mind was totally clear, totally focused on one thing. Hunting, killing, nothing else. He was not like a dog or a horse, animals in whom you can sense emotions and thought processes. Here it was only one way. Notice, focus, attack. So totally clear. No thinking about it, no reflection on it, no feelings around it, just the power itself. He was completely at home in his power and completely one with it.

Let me give an example of what might happen when I'm in my power (with the caveat that it's different for every person, both how each gets there and how it's expressed). I start from a place that is cold, clear, and seeing. I start by focusing outward. The energy condenses. The beam narrows. When this happens, my body doesn't exist. I am just focused energy.

A parallel experience happens to Arjuna, the warrior hero in the *Bhagavad Gita*. The teacher of the royal house wanted to test him and asked him to shoot a bird in a tree on a far riverbank.

The teacher asked, "Do you see the tree on the far bank?"

Arjuna replied, "No."

"Do you see the tree?"

"No."

"Do you see the branch the bird perches on?"

"No."

"What do you see?"

"I see only the bird."

"Tell me all that you can see."

"Sir, I cannot answer any of your questions. I can see nothing but the eye which I have to shoot... I feel that the eye and I have become one. There is no yawning gap between me and my target. My sight and the eye have become one in concentration."

(*The Story of Arjun*, Mantra on Internet.)

Where I differ from Brother Hawk is he is just focused outward, all the energy of his focus narrowly on scanning and on his prey. In contrast, after I focus out, then I bring the focus and energy back inside, so it expands. This expansion is from the heart. Now I'm in a place of compassion, loving and understanding myself. I gather up the loving heart energy.

When I'm there and totally focused, there's a sense of spacelessness, of infinity, of total connection to everything. At this moment power and balance, seeing and compassion all disappear and I'm just there. Everything seems to expand—time, seeing, consciousness. I look at the plant on the windowsill and see vibrations around it and in it. Others may see colors in an aura, but I see the energy running through the plant; then the plant disappears, and I see a ball of energy. I see the plant's connection to everything around it. Lines of energy come from the plant and connect to everything around it. It becomes more than a three-dimensional thing.

This stage reminds me of a poem by Li Po:
The birds have vanished into the sky,
and now the last cloud drains away.
We sit together, the mountain and me,
until only the mountain remains.
(Li Po, *Endless River*)

When I'm in that expanded place, nothing is violent. Here's an example from my sword class. After a session, one of my sparring partners said that there had been ten openings in his defense and I hadn't charged at any of them.

I said, "You know they're there, I know they're there. Do you really want me to let go?"

My partner hadn't come at me, so I felt no need to attack, felt safe. I just made an opening in his defense, smiled and went on. But it feels different at different times. During this sword class, I was mellow. A couple of weeks before, in the spear class, there was nothing anyone could do against me. My energy had been directed outward, so before the guys even thought about striking, they were hit. Sometimes if a partner strikes me, I'll just say, "Nice hit." Sometimes I'll zap out at him.

What does this have to do with balance? What I was learning from Brother Hawk was a completely new way of being in my power. He was fine being in his place of power, the cold, dark, clear hunter. He showed me how I could be okay in my place of power too, which for me meant going to that cold, dark, hyperfocused, clear space. But unlike him, also be loving at the same time.

At first, I thought being balanced meant to be balanced like a scale, to reach a middle space where love and ferocity, seeing and feeling, Being and Doing were equal. Next, I thought there was more movement involved, that I have different places of balance depending on where I am that day, depending on what the energy is like and what I am doing. Sometimes I moved toward the loving side, sometimes I moved toward the warrior side, keeping balanced in either case.

All this is correct. Now, I see another level. Your place of power may change with what you are doing, but the balance springs from your ability to love yourself when you are in that place of power.

Let me put it this way: Brother Hawk is 100 percent okay with being who he is. I realized that Brother Hawk had no fear at all of being in his place of power. He was totally focused and fine with being focused, hunting, killing. There was no anger, hate, or anything else. He was balanced and ready to hunt and kill his prey.

When I saw him fly out with total focus and clarity, I realized that I was not 100 percent okay with who I am when I am in my place of power. It's too scary. I've talked about my fear of hurting others or of being hurt. What lies below is the fear that when the power comes, I am not controlling it. It just is. I can't plan nor think ahead about what's going to happen. It just happens. I never know what's going to happen when I spar. If you try to get set for whatever's coming, you're a target, you're dead.

A patient from a western state called me the other day. I paused, but I didn't know what I was going to do or what was going to happen. I disappeared and saw her mother looming over her. I went forward into the darkness. Around me was an army of dark knights. There was also a tall, thin, black version of myself. There were entities that could harm, eat a soul, bring you to places you wouldn't want to go. I sent forces to move the mother away. Boom. It was fast, happened in a moment and then I was back.

This is scary. I have been afraid of hurting others when my power flashes out. So far, the energy has been right for what a particular situation needs, but I can't be sure that's always true. It helps that the warrior code is ingrained in me, there from previous lives. It would be inconceivable for me just to go and hit someone. Nor do I say, "He made me angry, so I'll just go after him." Still, there's no guarantee that I'm doing the right thing, especially since the energy and the situations are always changing. The Power is just what it is at a given moment. There are no fixed structures, no rules, no planning; the energy doesn't flow through me like a known substance. The energy is just what is at the particular moment.

I need to be like Brother Hawk. I need to put myself in my place of power and know it's okay for me to be there. It is where I belong. Otherwise, why would the Universe have taken me there? Yes, this is a little like an act of faith. As Wendell Berry said, "Sometimes it's easy to have faith and sometimes it isn't" (quoted in *The Sun*, July 2008, 14).

After meeting Brother Hawk, I began to do Ho'o Pono Pono to myself when I was in the place of power. This helped me clean any resistance (read, fear) to being in that place. It also balanced me. It somehow opened my heart at that same time.

So, what happens now is that when I disappear into the power and when I love that I am there, the Universe selects what balance point I need to be at. Sometimes I am just in that scary place of pure dark energy streaking out. Sometimes I am totally in my heart and holding someone in a loving way. And sometimes I am somewhere in between. I am wherever I am supposed to be at that time. Since I feel no resistance, since I totally accept what is happening, I do not build up any strange vibrations and so am able to stay in that place. The balance is the poise of being where I am at the moment.

The same holds true for people whose power is that of light and love. These are people who feel. Often what they feel first when they're with each other is not the person's love, but his or her pain. This isn't a bad thing; it's the way these people connect to another person's heart. It is how they become compassionate. But it isn't comfortable, to say the least. Most people want to get away from feeling another's pain as quickly as possible. In contrast, this feeling of another's pain and thus connecting with him or her is where healers get the most inspiration. However, if they stay totally focused on the pain of others and only reach out and try to help others, healers and feelers can end up getting depleted and hurt themselves. So, what they need to do is love themselves when they are in this powerful place of connecting—not back off, not wish they were anyone else, not fearing whether they'll hurt the other person. That's how healers can stay balanced and do their work best.

Just as healers first feel and connect with pain, when I see, what I see first is darkness. I would love to be in the light all the time, to love everything, but that is not the way it is for me. I need to be like Brother Hawk and be 100 percent okay with being in my Power. When I see darkness, and disappear, and summon up the dark forces, I need to be able to accept, love myself, love this place I am in, and love the dark power that flows from it. Only in this way is the energy balanced and only in this way can it be used for healing and not destruction.

The Gift

Throughout this book, I've been trying to tell the story of my ongoing effort to balance the dark energy in my life with the light. Earlier chapters describe how I came to use Being and Doing and Ho'o Pono Pono; and then, having learned from Brother Hawk, how I accepted my power of darkness and came to use focused waiting. This focused waiting is like what the *Tao Te Ching* calls "Wu Wei," no mind, creative emptiness. "Abiding in creative emptiness, one sees the wonders of the world" (sixth line of the *Tao Te Ching*, trans. Paul Gallagher).

Then, after all this learning and deepening, there came an experience that went beyond any that had come before, although the work and discipline that had gone into the earlier growth were necessary to ready me for this experience. Paradoxically, rather than focusing and using discipline, what I had to do here was let go, open to what was offered, and surrender to the grace of the Universe.

What follows is not going to be a conventional sequential narrative. It's a journey that happened to me. I'll try to make what happened as clear as I can, but it's a mystical experience, not a clear "this led to that" kind of sequence.

Let me set the stage. I have always felt sadness and darkness around me, darkness that has been there from birth. This darkness has come from memories of being in the Holocaust, of being killed in a gas chamber when I was just a teenager. These memories, profoundly fearful and painful, have been very much a part of me and have created a dark field around me. Throughout my whole life, I've tried to make peace with this part of me, to bring light to it, to understand why this past life memory was so strong. Nothing I have done has ever really worked.

Recently I was meeting with Gwendolin in my office. We have worked together for many years, and I respect her abilities. She is very psychic and has enormous intelligence and power. I don't remember how the subject of the Holocaust came up in our conversation, perhaps she was talking about someone she knew who had a connection to it. She already knew of my dark memories, so I mentioned them again.

Right away she went into a trance state. Her body started to sway, and her hands moved in circular patterns, very distinct movements she makes when she's having a psychic insight. She told me that she did not believe the memories of the Holocaust were mine.

"The experiences are not yours. They belong to someone else," she said with absolute certainty.

Now this was the third time a psychic person had told me this. The other two times, I heard what they said, I got the words, but when I looked, I couldn't see anything. If I can't see anything, the words alone don't shift my experience. I can't learn or make sense for myself of what I'm told.

This time, however, I did see and feel something, something amazing and transformative. When Gwendolin said the experience wasn't mine, I sensed an entity, an energy field moving away from me. I saw a flash of light, bright, and golden. Everything turned golden and I felt an enormous wave of compassion embrace me. I let it happen. All the darkness lifted. It felt as if the Bodhisattva of Compassion, Kuan Yin, had blessed me with her presence. I think Christians would call it the presence of Grace. The entity was saying goodbye to me as it moved off toward the light.

How did this feel? Hard to describe. While Gwendolin was saying, "The experiences are not yours," the whole thing happened between the words. Time stopped and everything happened in that space. Others have had similar experiences. Wordsworth talked about "spots of time" when he was simply in the awesome presence and power of nature, not conscious of himself as watching it, not aware of himself as a separate being in time.

I'm not claiming to be a figure like Wordsworth, but I was overcome. In the days that followed, the dark stuff was gone, the warm compassion remained. I was blessed with the entity's love and compassion for me, and I realized it was there to help me in some way I had yet to discover.

The entity was so beautiful when it left that I was sure it had to be a Bodhisattva, there to teach me something. I puzzled over what I was to learn, how to interpret this transformation. Also, I was puzzled whether I'd really had the experience of the Holocaust or whether it was the Boddhisattva's experience conveyed to me.

Whoever's memory it was, why would I need to experience the Holocaust at all? Maybe I was like Milarepa, who was powerful but who was so arrogant that his teacher had to help him learn humility. His teacher made him haul rocks and build a stone house on top of a hill. When Milarepa was finished, he was pleased with himself. His teacher said, "Very nice, but I made a mistake, the stone house needs to be on another hill."

Milarepa dragged stones up another hill and built another house. Tired, but proud of having accomplished the labor, he heard his teacher again say, "Mistake. Build it on the next hill."

This went on until Milarepa got the message: "Don't be arrogant and proud. Just do the task."

So maybe my experience of pain and suffering was to teach me not to be proud and arrogant as I certainly had been in earlier lives as a warrior and a shamanic warrior.

Or maybe the dark experience was to help me feel the pain of others' suffering.

At this point, I just didn't know.

A few weeks later, Gwendolin and I met again. We weren't expecting to talk about my earlier experience, because we had another topic we'd thought to address, but she suddenly went back into a trance state.

We saw a man who was in a Nazi concentration camp. He wore a striped uniform, was emaciated with big, big, eyes. Despite the horror, he seemed to have no fear but was very loving and had much compassion. He felt like some sort of Tsaddik, a good and wise man. He knew he was going to die soon and was not afraid, but he wanted to pass on his gift of love and compassion to someone, as it had been given to him. His lips didn't move, but I heard his voice right inside my head saying, "This is a very ancient gift that has been handed down to me."

He reached out through time and gave the gift to me in the same way that Buddhas and Bodisattvas pass on dharma transmission. The gift is not a thing, it's an experience that opens you. Dharma transmission is an experience of mind to mind, an energetic exchange. Think of downloading a file onto a computer. Or think of Paul's experience on the road to Damascus when "a light from heaven flashed about him. And he fell to the ground," and the Lord spoke to him (Acts, 9:3-4).

There was no sense of the experience's being Jewish or Christian or Buddhist or any other specific religion. It seemed like pure energy, like being embraced by the Universe. The only way I can articulate the experience is to say that I was one with Being, was able to experience the unity.

This experience felt like letting go of something, something that had to fall away so that I could connect to something, an opening up, so that some energy could be transmitted to me. Something lets go and then you're in a different place, not here.

When I was with him, I asked him why I'd had to undergo the years of darkness and painful awareness of the camp. Maybe to balance my gift of power, I wondered. He said I needed to pass a test. He needed to see whether I could handle the darkness and pain before he passed on his gift to me. After he said this, he dissolved into light and was gone.

I guess somehow, I passed the test. I have no idea: why me? The man who brought me a gift of grace had been with me all my life, but I hadn't been ready before then to receive what he had for me. The best I can figure is that all the work I'd done had gotten me to a place where I could have that experience and use it wisely. I've always been able to send focused energy. Now I think I can send grace too.

My experience reminded me of Ueshiba. In Chapter One, on Being and Doing, I said that Ueshiba had learned to balance these two modes. I think that he was able to do so because this wild, ferocious warrior had an enlightenment in which he experienced the love in the Universe. He wrote,

> Above all, one must unite one's heart with that of the gods. The essence of God is love, an all-pervading love that reaches every corner of the Universe. If one is not united to God, the Universe cannot be harmonized (Mitchell, *Abundant Peace*, 112).

I've been asked, "Really, why did this happen?" I don't know. "Exactly what is the gift?" I don't know. "Why me?" I don't know. Whatever the answers (or maybe there aren't any), it's probably not a coincidence that something else was going on at that time, something which also involved a being who had been with me for a while before I was ready to receive.

Rhiannon

A week before this all started, I was doing one of my regular Sunday morning workouts. They were demanding, doing body weight movements on the floor in thirty-second bursts. As usual I was concentrating in silence.

My younger son came into the room, and I mentioned to him that I'd read a *New York Times* article saying people perform better when they exercise to music than when they don't. He got out his iPod and of the thousands of songs he had on it, he culled three hundred "old school" songs for me. He shuffled them, and the first song up was the seventies favorite "Rhiannon" by Fleetwood Mac.

I had liked the song when it first came out, but this time when I heard it, I had to stop exercising. The music seemed to go on and on as if time were still; the song kept reverberating in my head as if I were alone with it out of time.

The song kept after me. I needed to learn why it had shifted my experience of time. I had no idea who Rhiannon was, but my understanding of the song's persistence was that she was surely with me. I had to find out who she was.

My most immediate way of finding out about someone is to focus my energy and attention and then wait until I see, get an image. As I focused, I did see her. She was dressed in Celtic garb, a flowing green gown and a green cape with gold trim. Holding back her auburn hair, she wore a wide headband of green fabric with gold Celtic patterns. She rode a white horse, white like alabaster or marble, whiteness with a white quality all the way through it. Around her was a golden glow that pulsed. Surrounding her, dark against the golden light, were birds, small ones like sparrows, bigger ones like robins, bluebirds, and crows.

Curious to find out more about her, I turned to Google and reference books. They told me that Rhiannon was the Celtic goddess of the moon, and that the horse was her symbol of both earthly and otherworldly power. Most sources agreed that, as in my vision, she always rode a white horse and always had birds around her. They were birds of healing. Another legend connected her with Vivienne, who gave Excalibur to Arthur, enabling him to become king and to form Camelot.

As the days went by, I felt as if Rhiannon kept connecting me to horses, encouraging me to ride. There weren't words, as had been the case with the Tsaddik, more just a kind of knowing that this was what she meant. I just knew in my head she wanted me to ride. I don't know how I knew, I just did.

Now, I do know how to ride a horse at a beginner's level, and my wife, who is an excellent rider, and I had actually once owned a horse. But I had some doubts about what Rhiannon wanted. Not long before, while on vacation, I'd tried to get on a horse and had been terrified, a global fear like a panic attack. I'd gotten off very fast.

Though puzzled, I still loved and trusted the light and compassion around Rhiannon. Finally, she too gave me a gift. The Boddhisatva's gift described in an earlier chapter had been like an experience of enlightenment or satori. Rhiannon's transmission was more like the shamanic experience in which one receives a certain power or powers. In both cases, however, I needed to be ready to receive what was given.

When I go into the realms where Rhiannon rides, I see her on her great white horse galloping over a dark plain with clouds gray and black and silver streaking above her. At first, there was just this, but as I spent more time with her, I realized there was a large, totally black stallion running with her. He was such pure ebony black that I hadn't seen him at first. I realized this horse was for me to ride, to ride in the other realms, to ride for power, to balance the dark and the white.

I rode the black horse beside Rhiannon every day. The air around us was pitch black, but though I couldn't see him, I could feel the horse underneath me, could feel his power.

As I rode with Rhiannon, she said I needed to face my fear. To do so, she directed me to get on a physical horse in the ordinary world. Riding a physical horse would simultaneously become riding the spiritual horse.

Okay, I know that sounds confusing. Let me try to explain. As I said in the chapter on discipline, repeating a physical form often enough and attentively enough can free me to gain mastery. And mastery is not just a physical skill, it involves "being in the zone," being free of awareness of self, being just the spirit accomplishing. Remember how in *Zen in the Art of Archery*, the accomplished bowman becomes the arrow focusing on and meeting the target. When I get lost in doing Tai Chi, I am doing the physical form and the spiritual move at the same time.

Or to put the matter another way, riding a physical horse could become riding a spiritual horse. Rhiannon first led me to ride the spiritual horse. I could ride the spiritual horse in meditation and use it to take me to places that heal, that work on the heart. But the point is to do healing and heart work in the ordinary world too. That is the Mahayana ideal.

There is a spectrum from the spiritual or psychic to the physical. Everything is in both simultaneously. Those who see auras can see levels of energy starting with the physical body but also rising in layers upon layers to the level of pure energy. True, people can be at one end or the other of the spectrum, either totally engaged in the material world or off entirely in the spiritual like mystics who can't function in the everyday. People at each extreme of the spectrum ignore what they're missing; people along the spectrum have glimpses of both. What I've worked hard on is being in all simultaneously.

I was still afraid to get on a worldly horse, but I knew I was going to have to.

Death Grip on the Pommel

As I rode with Rhiannon, she directed me. The first thing she told me I had to do was face fear. The way to do so, she said, was to get on a physical horse in the everyday, ordinary realm. She was clear about this. My reaction was to be terrified. I was afraid of being out of my element; I was afraid that because of an injury, my left leg didn't have enough strength to grip a horse's flank; I was afraid of being out of control, up off the ground on a large beast. My fear even seemed to go beyond such reasons; the panic was so intense and outside of me it almost felt as if it were not just mine but some kind of being feeding on me.

But this was the point: she said I had to do something that would get me out of my comfort zone. I had to face the fear, she said, for going through such fear, fear that overwhelms, opens new possibilities.

Okay, I took a deep breath and tried to figure out a way to ride the horse so it wouldn't give me any outs or evasions. I couldn't go to the ocean because that was familiar, nor could I go to the mountains because then I'd just go up and meditate. I do like challenges, so here's what I came up with: for our next vacation, my wife and I took a trip to an Arizona horse ranch in the northern Sonora desert.

Talk about being out of my comfort zone. Here I was, a northern woods, mountain, and ocean boy in the desert. No trees, seemingly limitless horizon, red dirt and sand, hills and deep canyons. It was like being on the moon.

I'd never ridden horses in wide open spaces before. I'm not used to even being in a wide-open environment without trees to give a sense of comfort and enclosure. I don't like heights, and because I'm big, the wranglers put me on big high horses. I like my feet planted firmly on the ground and being in control, not relying on some animal.

Looking at my fear in long meditation every morning and reminding myself that I was a warrior and that Rhiannon wanted me to do this, I rode three to five hours a day. The wranglers would saddle up the horses and lead my wife and me into the desert. Being totally out of my element, I had to face the unknown and live with being out of control.

It helped that I could use a western saddle, which is wide and has a pommel. Riding on the flat was not a problem. Riding uphill was not a problem. Going downhill was terrifying. Suddenly, the horse would go down the steep side of a canyon and there'd be nothing in front of me but seventy to a hundred feet straight on down.

My tactic was to lean way back, stick my legs out straight as if to brace myself, and hold the pommel in a death grip with both hands. After a few days of watching me torture myself, one of the cowboys said to me, "You have to have faith in your horse."

After that I could let go, trust my horse, not be afraid, and go down the steepness into the depths.

Works Cited

Berry, Wendell. Quoted in *The Sun*, July 2008: 14.

Damasio, Antonio. Descartes' *Error: Emotion, Reason, and the Human Brain*. New York: Penguin, 2005.

Dowd, Maureen. *New York Times*. 19 October, 2010.

Gladwell, Malcolm. *Outliers: The Story of Success*. New York: Little Brown, 2008.

Herrigel, Eugan and Daisetz T. Suzuki. *Zen in the Art of Archery*. Trans. R.F.C. Hull. New York, NY: Vintage Spiritual Classics, 1999.

Kant, Immanuel. Groundwork *of the Metaphysics of Morals*. Ed. Mary Gregor. Cambridge Texts in the History of Philosophy. Cambridge: Cambridge University Press, 2007.

Li Po. In *Classical Chinese Poetry*. Trans. and ed. David Hinton. New York: Farrar, Straus and Giroux, 2008.

Myerson, John, and Judith Robbins. *Voices from the Other Side of the Couch*: *A Warrior's View of Shamanic Healing*. Framingham, MA: LifeArts Press, 2008.

Stevens, John. Abundant Peace: *the Biography of Morihei Ueshiba*, Founder of Akido. Boston: Shambala, 1987.

____. *The Sword of No Sword: Life of the Master Warrior Teshu*. Boston: Shambala, 1989.

"The Story of Arjun." Mantra on Net. The Realm of Divinity. Cerebrum Tech., 2005.

Vitale, Joe, and Ihaleakala Hew Len. *Zero Limits: The Secret Hawaiian System for Wealth, Health, Peace and More.* Hoboken, NJ: John Wiley, 2007.

Suggested Readings

Amberger, J. Christoph. *The Secret History of the Sword*. Burbank, CA: Unique Publications, 1998.

Bates, Brian. *The Real Middle Earth*. New York: Palgrave MacMillan, 2002.

____. *Way of Wyrd*. New York: Harpercollins, 1992.

Bear, Jaya. Amazon Magic, *The Life Story of Ayahuasquero and Shaman Don Agustin Rivas Vasquez*. Taos, NM: Colibri Publishing, 2000.

Berry, Wendell. Quoted in *The Sun*. July 2008: 14.

Bhagavadgita. Trans. Stephen Mitchell. New York: Three Rivers Press, 2000.

Blofeld, John. *Taoism: The Road to Immortality*. Boston: Shambhala, 1978.

____ Trans. *The Zen Teaching of Huang Po*. New York, NY: Grove Press, 1958.

Bolelli, Daniele. *On the Warrior's Path: Philosophy, Fighting, and Martial Arts Mythology*. Berkeley, CA: Frog Ltd, 2003.

Bolen, Jean Shinoda. *Goddesses in Everywoman*. New York: Harper and Row, 1984.

———. *Gods in Everyman*. New York: Harper and Row, 1989.

Campbell, Joseph. *The Power of Myth*. New York: Doubleday, 1988.

Canizares, Raul. *Walking with the Night: The Afro-Cuban World of Santeria*. Rochester, VT: Destiny Books, 1993.

Capra, Fritjof. *The Tao of Physics*. Boston: Shambhala, 1975.

Castaneda, Carlos. *Journey to Ixtalan*. New York: Simon and Schuster, 1972.

———. *Tales of Power*. New York: Simon and Schuster, 1974.

Chuang Tsu. *Inner Chapters*. Trans. Gia-Fu Feng and Jane English. New York: Vintage, 1974.

Dalai Lama. *The Universe in a Single Atom: The Convergence of Science and Spirituality*. New York: Morgan Road Books, 2005.

Damasio, Antonio. *Descartes' Error: Emotion, Reason, and the Human Brain*. New York: Penguin, 2005.

Danos, Kosta. *The Magus of Java*. Rochester VT: Inner Traditions, 2000.

Deng Ming-Dao. *Scholar Warrior: An Introduction to the Tao in Everyday Life*. New York, NY: Harper Collins, 1990.

Dowd, Maureen. *New York Times*. 19 October 2010.

Dunn, James. *Wisdom of the Soul: The Kabbalah of Rabbi Isaac Luria*. Newburyport, MA: Weiser Books, 2008.

Eliot, George. *Middlemarch*. Oxford: Oxford University Press, 1996.

Estes, Clarissa Pinkola. *Women Who Run with the Wolves*. New York: Ballantine Books, 1992.

Fulford, Robert. *Dr. Fulford's Touch of Life*. New York: Pocket Books, 1996.

Gallagher, Paul. *Drawing Silk: Masters' Secrets for Successful T'ai Chi Practice*. Fairview, NC: Total Tai Chi, 2007.

Gladwell, Malcolm. *Outliers: The Story of Success*. New York: Little Brown, 2008.

Goodman, Felicitas D. *Where the Spirits Ride the Wind: Trance Journeys and Other Ecstatic Experiences*. Bloomington, IN: Indiana University Press, 1990.

———— and Nana Nauwald. *Ecstatic Trance: New Ritual Body Postures*. Havelte, Holland: Binkey Kok Publications, 2003.

Hanh, Thich Nhat. *Old Path White Clouds: Walking in the Footsteps of the Buddha*. Berkeley, CA: Parallax Press, 1991.

Harner, Michael. *The Way of the Shaman*. San Francisco and New York: Harper and Row, 1980.

Hayward, Ray. *Lessons with Master Liang: T'ai Chi, Philosophy and Life*. St. Paul, MN: Shu-Kuang Press, 2011.

Herrigel, Eugan, and Daisetz T Suzuki. *Zen in the Art of Archery*. Trans. R.F.C. Hull. New York, NY: Vintage Spiritual Classics, 1999.

Hesse, Hermann. *Siddhartha*. New York: New Directions, 1951.

Hildegard of Bingen. *Book of Divine Works*. Ed. Matthew Fox. Santa Fe: Bear and Co., 1987.

Hoff, Benjamin. *The Tao of Pooh*. New York: Penguin, 1982.

Kant, Immanuel. *Groundwork of the Metaphysics of Morals*. Ed. Mary Gregor. Cambridge Texts in the History of Philosophy. Cambridge: Cambridge University Press, 2007.

Kapleau, Philip. *The Three Pillars of Zen*. Boston: Beacon Press, 1965.

Keeney, Bradford. *Bushman Shaman: Awakening the Spirit through Ecstatic Dance*. Rochester VT: Destiny Books, 2005.

Kottler, Jeffrey, and Jon Carlson. *American Shaman*. New York: Brunner-Routledge, 2004.

Krishnamurti. *On Fear*. New York: HarperOne, 1995.

Lame Deer, Archie Fire. *Gift of Power*. Santa Fe: Bear and Co., 1994.

Lao Tsu. *Tao Te Ching*. Trans. Gia-Fu and Jane English. New York: Vintage Books, 1972.

Lawlor, Robert. *Voices of the First Day: Awakening in the Aboriginal Dreamtime*. Rochester, VT: Inner Traditions, 1991.

Li Po. In *Classical Chinese Poetry*. Trans. and ed. David Hinton New York: Farrar, Straus and Giroux, 2008.

Markides, Kyriacos C. *The Magus of Sgtrovolos*. New York: Penguin, 1985.

Matthews, Caitlin and John. *Walkers between the Worlds: The Western Mysteries from Shaman to Magus*. Rochester VT: Inner Traditions, 2003.

Mountain, Marian. *The Zen Environment: The Impact of Zen Meditation*. Bantam Books: NY, 1983.

Musashi, Miyamoto. *A Book of Five Rings*. Woodstock, NY: Overlook Press, 1982.

Myerson, John, and Robert Greenebaum. *Riding the Spirit Wind*. Framingham, MA: LifeArts Press, 2003.

Myerson, John, and Judith Robbins. *Voices from the Other Side of the Couch: A Warrior's View of Shamanic Healing*. Framingham: LifeArts Press, 2008.

Nan, H. C. *Tao and Longevity: Mind-Body Transformation*. Newburyport, MA: Weiser, 1984.

Neihardt, John G. *Black Elk Speaks: Being the Life Story of a Holy Man of the Oglala Sioux*. Lincoln, NE: University of Nebraska Press, 1961.

Olson, Stuart Alve. *Steal My Art: The Life and Times of T'ai Chi Master TT Liang*. Berkeley, CA: North Atlantic Books, 2002.

Porter, Bill. *Road to Heaven: Encounters with Chinese Hermits*. Berkeley, CA: Counterpoint, 1993.

———. *Zen Baggage, A Pilgrimage to China*. Berkeley, CA: Counterpoint, 2009.

Profiles in Healing Series. Ed. Bradford Keeney. Philadelphia: Ringing Rocks Press.

> *Balians: Traditional Healers of Bali*
> *Gary Holy Bull: Lakota Yuwipi Man*
> *Guarani Shamans of the Forest*
> *Hands of Faith: Healers of Brazil*

Ikuko Osumi, Sensei: Japanese Master of Seiki Jutsu
Kalahari Bushmen Healers
Ropes to God: Experiencing the Bushman Spiritual Universe
Shakers of St. Vincent
Vusamazulu Credo Mutwa: Sulu High Sanusi
Walking Thunder: Dine Medicine Women

Red Pine. Trans. *The Zen Teaching of Bodhidharma*. New York, NY: North Point Press, 1987.

____. *Lao-Tzu's Tao Te Ching*. Port Townsend, WA: Copper Canyon Press, 2009.

Ritchie, Mark Andrew. *Spirit of the Rain Forest: A Yanomamo Shaman's Story*. Chicago: Island Lake Press, 2000.

Salzberg, Sharon. Lovingkindness: *The Revolutionary Art of Happiness*. Boston: Shambhala, 2008.

Smith, Philip. *Walking Through Walls*. New York, NY: Atura Books, 2008.

Some, Malidoma. *Of Water and the Spirit*. New York: Tarcher, 1994.

Soygul Rinpoche. *The Tibetan Book of Living and Dying*. San Francisco: Harper, 1984.

Starhawk. *The Spiral Dance*. Boston: Beacon, 1978.

Steinsaltz, Adin. *The Thirteen Petalled Rose: A Discourse on the Essence of Jewish Existence and Belief.* New York: Basic Books, 2006.

Stevens, John. *Abundant Peace: The Biography of Morihei Ueshiba, Founder of Akido*. Boston: Shambhala, 1987.

_____. *The Sword of No Sword: Life of the Master Warrior Tesshu.* Boston: Shambhala, 1989.

"*The Story of Arjun.*" Mantra on Net. The Realm of Divinity. Cerebrum Tech. 2005.

Stozzi-Heckler, Richard. In *Search of the Warrior Spirit:* Teaching Awareness Discipline to the Green Berets. Berekeley: North Atlantic Books, 2003.

Suzuki, Shunryu. *Zen Mind, Beginner's Mind.* New York and Tokyo: Weatherhill, 1970.

Tart, Charles. *Transpersonal Psychologies: Perspectives on the Mind from Seven Great Spiritual Traditions.* New York: Harpercollins, 1992.

Taylor, Jill Bolte. *My Stroke of Insight: A Brain Scientist's Personal Journey.* New York, NY: Viking, 2006.

Trungpa, Chogyam. Shambhala: *The Sacred Path of the Warrior.* Boston: Shambhala, 1984.

Van der Wettering, Janwillem. *After Zen.* New York: St. Martin's Press, 1999.

_____. *The Empty Mirror.* Boston: Houghton Mifflin, 1973.

_____. *A Glimpse of Nothingness.* Boston: Houghton Mifflin, 1975.

Vitale, Joe, and Ihaleakala Hew Len. *Zero Limits, The Secret Hawaiian System for Wealth, Health, Peace and More.* Hoboken, NJ: John Wiley, 2007.

Waddell, Norman. Trans. *The Spiritual Autobiography of Zen Master Hakuin.* Boston: Shambhala, 2001.

Welch, Holmes. *Taoism: The Parting of the Way*. Boston: Beacon, 1965.

Whitaker, Kay. *The Reluctant Shaman*. New York: Harpercollins, 1991.

Wilson, Carol Ann. *Stillpoint of the Turning World: The Life of Gia-fu Feng*. Portland, OR: Amber Lotus Publications, 2009.

Wolf, Fred Alan. *The Eagle's Quest: A Physicist Finds the Scientific Truth at the Heart of the Shamanic World*. New York: Touchstone, 1991.

The Zen Teaching of Huang Po. Trans. John Blofeld. New York: Grove Press, 1958.

About the Authors

John G. Myerson, Ph.D., Lic. Ac., is a graduate of Harvard College and the New England School of Acupuncture. He received his Doctorate in Psychology from The Union Institute. He practices shamanic healing, psychotherapy, and Oriental medicine, and is the founder of the LifeArts Center for Healing and Shamanic Studies in Framingham, Massachusetts. John has studied, practiced, and taught Zen, yoga, Taoist cultivation, martial arts, and shamanic practices for over forty years.

Judith Robbins, A.B., M.A.T., studied philosophy and literature at Harvard University. As well as teaching in these areas for over forty years, she has also studied, practiced, and taught meditation, t'ai chi, yoga, and shamanic healing for many years. In addition to co-authoring *Voices from the Other Side of the Couch* with John Myerson, she co-authored the sixth edition (and earlier editions) of *Writing a Research Paper*, published in 2008 by Wayside Press.

www.ingramcontent.com/pod-product-compliance
Lightning Source LLC
Chambersburg PA
CBHW072050290426
44110CB00014B/1618